The Pocket Essential

AUDREY HEPBURN

First published in Great Britain 2004 by
Pocket Essentials, PO Box 394, Harpenden, Herts, AL5 1XJ, UK

Distributed in the USA by Trafalgar Square Publishing,
PO Box 257, Howe Hill Road, North Pomfret, Vermont 05053

A CIP catalogue record for this book is available from the British Library.

ISBN 1-903047-67-6

2 4 6 8 10 9 7 5 3 1

Book typeset by Wordsmith Solutions Ltd
Printed and bound by Cox & Wyman

For Mum
- who'll probably be on the rampage when she reads this.

Fashion advice for every woman who will listen:

Be dressed for what you are doing.

Have the right accessories.

Don't wear your clothes too tight. A dress should be tight enough to show you're a woman and loose enough to prove you're a lady.

Edith Head,
Fashion Chief of Paramount Pictures,
as quoted in *The Dress Doctor*.

Acknowledgements

My thanks go to: Joy and David Cheshire, Greg Nunes, Mike Mantell, Erica Ying Ying Cheung, Tze Cheng, Louise Scrivens, Kathleen Luckey and John Ashbrook.

In Memory

In the last month of writing this book (June/July 2003), four key people connected with Audrey Hepburn sadly passed away. I would like to dedicate this book in their memory...

Gregory Peck, her *Roman Holiday* co-star (1916-2003)
Buddy Ebsen, her *Breakfast At Tiffany's* co-star (1908-2003)
Alexander Walker, her biographer (1930-2003)
And, although they never worked together, we must pay tribute to the other late great Hepburn, Katharine (1907-2003)

CONTENTS

1. ...And She Lived Happily Ever After?

Once upon a time there was a beautiful princess...

Audrey Hepburn has remained an enduring icon of the silver screen. Almost every week the national press uses a picture of Audrey to illustrate articles on subjects as diverse as the power of the little black dress, film stars who encouraged people to smoke and how to crack an egg. The list of current Hollywood stars who are the next Audrey Hepburn is endless. Recent additions (to name only a few) have included Gwyneth Paltrow, Natalie Portman, Halle Berry and Penelope Cruz. Early in her career, Audrey was the face on Lux Soap and Crookes' Lacto-Calamine advertisements. Now she's seen selling Longine's exclusive Swiss watches and Gordon's Gin.

What is it about Audrey Hepburn that is so magical and transcendent?

Audrey spent her childhood between Belgium and England. She spoke English faultlessly and her early successes were on the London stage and in British movies, but her looks were not those of the English Rose, nor did she look like the platinum blondes so prevalent in Hollywood in the early 1950s. Her Europeanism, looks, figure and manner set her apart and created a whole new look that was emulated the world over. She was a paradox: Innocence with sexiness, naiveté with worldliness. She was modern, classic, sophisticated and above all - fresh.

During her forty-four-year career, Audrey only appeared in twenty-six films and never made more than two films a year. Her desire for, and devotion to, her own family was evident throughout her acting career as she believed that her family should always come first. She spent much of her adult life living in Europe, avoiding the Hollywood lifestyle, favouring films that were set or filmed in Europe. Of those twenty-six films, Audrey was the star of only nineteen, but yet they include some of the greatest films of all time: *Roman Holiday, Sabrina Fair, Funny Face, The Nun's Story, Breakfast At Tiffany's, Charade, My Fair Lady* and *How To Steal A Million*. Those half-dozen or so classic films remain with us as a record of a young girl, who grew from a princess in William Wyler's 1953 *Roman Holiday,* to an angel in Steven Spielberg's 1989 *Always.*

But she wasn't just an angel on-screen. In the last years of her life she fulfilled that role off-screen as well, when she became a Goodwill Ambassador for UNICEF in 1988. The Red Cross had saved her life at the end of the Second Word War. Ill and malnourished, she received aid from them and she always remained closely involved in charities, especially those that provided care for children. Her son, Sean Hepburn Ferrer, is now Chairman of the Audrey Hepburn Children's Fund.

Audrey was born Edda Kathleen Hepburn van Heemstra in Brussels on 4 May 1929. (Brussels is most commonly published regarding Audrey's place of birth. However, in a recently published book by David Seabrook, he claims that Audrey was born in Folkstone, Kent.) Her mother was Baroness Ella van Heemstra, part of the Dutch aristocracy. Her grandfather was Baron Aarnoud van Heemstra who held the post of Governor of Dutch Guiana under personal invitation from Queen Wilhelmina. One of her aunts, Baroness Marianne van Heemstra, was lady-in-waiting to Princess Juliana, who later became Queen.

Ella's first marriage resulted in two sons: Ian and Alexander. When she met and married Audrey's father, Joseph Hepburn-Ruston, she was determined to keep the family together and devoted herself to her children. It was not to be a happy marriage and Joseph walked out on the family when Audrey was six years old. Mystery surrounds his life, but it is well documented that he was a member of Sir Oswald Mosely's Union of Fascists. He was branded a traitor and spent the war years in an Internment Camp on the Isle of Man. Alexander Walker's biography, *Audrey - Her Real Story*, goes into great detail about Audrey's relationship with her father and, in his revised and expanded 2000 edition, includes a postscript in which he details subsequent research into Audrey's father. David Seabrook in his book, *All The Devils Are Here*, on a tour of Kentish towns, adds some further information on the subject.

Audrey's early childhood would shape her life and career. When the Second World War broke out, Audrey's mother took the family back to Arnhem, Holland, believing they would be safe there. However, when the Germans invaded and Hitler's forces occupied Arnhem, they seized the van Heemstra family fortune. Audrey's half-brother was sent to a labour camp and one of her uncles was shot by a firing squad. By the end of the war, Audrey, undernourished and suffering from anaemia and asthma, had developed oedema and hepatitis. The anaemia meant that she found it impossible to put on weight in her later life, causing severe concerns over her health and even her ability to carry a child.

Audrey recovered and once restrictions on travel were lifted, with £35 in their pockets, Audrey and her mother moved to London where Audrey enrolled at Madame Rambert's Ballet School. However, her height, weak health and limited funds forced her to leave the school and find a job.

Concerns over her weight and figure plagued her. Early on in her career she recalls overhearing a producer say, 'Heck, if I wanted to look at bones, I could always have my foot X-rayed.'

Her big break came in West End revues, which she did back-to-back with a cabaret show at Ciro's night-club. It was there that a producer spotted her and cast her in a small part in her first British Movie, *One Wild Oat*. A series of other small parts followed; the most memorable were in *The Lavender Hill Mob* and *Laughter In Paradise*.

Larger speaking parts in *Young Wives' Tale* and *The Secret People* brought newspaper and magazine coverage. As did her engagement in 1952 to James (later Lord) Hanson, the son of a wealthy Huddersfield road-haulage tycoon and an industrialist in his own right. But despite the announcement in *The Times*, the marriage was not to be as Audrey's career soon took off and Hanson just didn't fit into her new schedule. By the time she was performing in the Broadway production of *Gigi*, the romance was faltering. When she had finished her first Hollywood film, *Roman Holiday*, it was over. Audrey called the wedding off two weeks before it was due to take place. The wedding gown, which Audrey had spent six months designing with the Italian courtiers Fontana, was given away.

Paramount had been on tenterhooks after they had signed her for the role of the princess in *Roman Holiday*, until *Gigi* opened. If Audrey was a success, they would have a Broadway star in their film; if she failed, they would have an unknown European actress. Audrey succeeded so much, Gregory Peck, who was a huge star and entitled to solo billing above the title, begged the studio to place Audrey's name alongside his. He feared he would be a laughing stock as he knew she was going to steal the film from under him and win an Oscar - she did both.

In 1954, she met two men that would have a major impact on her life. Audrey's career was in ascendance when she met Mel Ferrer at the London launch of *Roman Holiday*. He was fifteen years older than Audrey, twice married and had four children. Her friends and family were concerned by their blossoming romance. His career had been a stop/start affair and when they had met, had all but stopped. Her success on Broadway in *Gigi* back-to-back with *Roman Holiday* had firmly established her as a star. No sooner had they met and fallen in love, he began to get a reputation as a 'Svengali' figure, manipulating Audrey's career and flying on her coat-tails. Rumours began of him 'blackmailing' producers: if they wanted Audrey, they would have to hire him as well.

The second meeting came during the pre-production of her second Hollywood film, *Sabrina Fair*, and would be one of the most important relationships of her life - her friendship with Hubert de Givenchy, the French fashion designer. They first met and worked together when he was hired to design Audrey's Paris wardrobe for *Sabrina Fair*. He described her as 'the perfect model ... she had the ideal face and figure, with her long slim body and swan-like neck.' The two men would come together when Mel Ferrer negotiated Audrey's contract for *Funny Face*. In it, it stated that she would keep her wardrobe of clothes designed for the film by Givenchy. From there he insisted that all contracts would have a Givenchy clause in them - wherever possible, he would design her costumes on-screen.

Audrey's and Givenchy's careers would become inseparable. He created that Audrey Hepburn look on which whole books have been written (*Audrey Style*), and he had the perfect advertisement for his *haute couture*. Their friendship and business relationship continued throughout her career; he was still designing her costumes in her 1980s films and off-screen he also continued designing clothes for her.

Sadly, her relationship with Mel Ferrer would not prove so enduring. They appeared on-stage together in *Ondine* in 1954, and on film in 1956 in *War And Peace* and she relied on him for making business decisions and choosing her roles. However, her most successful films were those with which he had little or no involvement. Their relationship became more and more strained as her career eclipsed his. Despite a number of miscarriages, they had one son, Sean Ferrer, in 1960, but her longed-for child did not equal a happy family and in 1967 their marriage was over. The following year, she married psychiatrist Andrea Dotti. Determined that her family would take priority, she gave up acting and became a 'housewife', bringing up Sean and their son Luca, who was born in 1970. She returned to the screen in 1976 with *Robin And Marian,* but it was not a happy experience and she made only a few films over the next thirteen years.

In 1988, she became a Special Goodwill Ambassador to UNICEF, filling a post that Danny Kaye had enjoyed for the last twenty years of his life. The children she visited did not know who she was; just a nice woman who would listen and cuddle them. Over the next five years she made fifty trips for UNICEF. Her fame brought the TV cameras and photographers, which ensured that UNICEF would get maximum exposure for its causes.

Following her separation (they would not divorce until 1982) from Dr Andrea Dotti, she met Dutchman Robert Wolders in 1981. He had recently been widowed following his wife Merle Oberon's losing fight to cancer. Robert and Audrey shared a great deal in common, having grown up in Holland a mere thirty miles apart. They remained together until she died in Tolochenaz in 1993.

Now, more than a decade after her death, Audrey remains as popular as ever. A museum converted from a two-room school in 1996 in the Swiss village of Tolochenaz where she had lived for twenty-eight years has attracted tens of thousands of visitors each year and has turned this sleepy part of Switzerland into a major tourist attraction.

A few of Audrey's contemporaries are nearly as famous, or notorious, today. Some are more famous, or notorious, than they were when they were alive, but none has managed to retain the timeless magnetic allure of an actress who, right from the start (as Cecil Beaton noted in this diary on 23 July 1953), was 'a new type of beauty: huge mouth, flat Mongolian features, heavily painted eyes, a coconut coiffure, long nails without varnish, a wonderfully lithe figure, a long neck ... In a flash I discovered A.H. is chock-a-block with sprite-like charm ... [and] a sort of waifish, poignant sympathy.'

2. And Introducing ... Audrey Hepburn

Nederlands In 7 Lessen
Dutch In 7 Lessons (1948)

Cast: Koes Koen (Wam Heskes/George), A Viruly (Air Pilot), Audrey Hepburn (Air Hostess).

Crew: Director: Charles Huguenot van der Linden. Producer: H M Josephson. Filmed in the Netherlands. Dutch. 79 minutes and 38 minutes.

Story: Despite its title, this film is not an educational video but a Dutch feature film about a girl-crazy cameraman (Koes Koen) who has a week to make a travelogue of Holland.

Background: Filmed in the Netherlands, this is Audrey Hepburn's first screen appearance as a sexy young KLM air hostess.

Made for the Rank Film company, the two film-makers (Charles Huguenot van der Linden and H M Josephson) cobbled together this film, mostly using aerial shots of Amsterdam from their archives. They filmed short sequences on the ground about an English cameraman making a travelogue, constantly tempted by the beautiful Dutch maidens.

Two versions of the film exist. In the longer version shown in the Netherlands, Audrey is seen twice: first as a pretty young thing skipping down the road, into whom the cameraman bumps; and the second time sees her as the air hostess waving him goodbye. In the 38-minute truncated version shown in the UK, only Audrey's air hostess role survived.

Accounts vary on how Audrey got the role. Following the war and the return of Audrey's health, Audrey began studying ballet once again. One account reveals that the producer and director visited Madame Sonia Gaskell's studios in Amsterdam, where Audrey was studying, looking for a suitable young girl. There, they spotted Audrey and cast her in the small role. The other relies on her family connections rather than her natural talent: a mutual acquaintance of the van Heemstras and the director van Der Linden arranged for Audrey's audition.

Regardless of how she came to be cast, her three days' filming gave her a taste of the movie life, but it wasn't enough of a life to lure her away from her grand passion - ballet. The following year, with restrictions in air travel lifted between the Netherlands and England, Audrey and her mother left for England where Audrey studied ballet with the famous Dame Marie Rambert.

One Wild Oat (1951)

Cast: Robertson Hare (Humphrey Proudfoot), Stanley Holloway (Alfred Gilbey), Constance Lorne (Mrs Proudfoot), Vera Pearce (Mrs Gilbey), June Sylvaine (Cherrie Proudfoot), Andrew Crawford (Fred Gilbey), Irene Handl (Audrey Cuttle), Sam Costa (Mr Pepys), Robert Moreton (Throstle), Charles Grove (Charles), Joan Rice (Annie), Audrey Hepburn (Hotel Regency Receptionist).

Crew: Director: Charles Saunders. Producer: John Croydon. Written by Vernon Sylvaine and Lawrence Huntington based on Sylvaine's play. Filmed in England. UK. 78 minutes.

Story: The shy and respectable solicitor, Humphrey Proudfoot (Robertson Hare), is distraught when his daughter, Cherrie (June Sylvaine), announces that she is in love with the young and handsome Fred Gilbey (Andrew Crawford), especially when he discovers that he is the son of neighbouring gambler and greyhound owner, Alfred Gilbey (Stanley Holloway).

Without having met Fred, her father is against the wedding and forbids his daughter from entering this unsuitable marriage. As the wives get to know each other, the husbands carry out a series of underhand ploys in an effort to outwit each other.

Blackmail is the name of the game. As Humphrey hires a private investigator to dig into the Gilbey family, Alfred is forced to try to conceal a series of ill-timed love affairs. Phoning the Hotel Regency, the charming receptionist (Audrey Hepburn) agrees to help. But it's too late. The private investigator confronts Alfred and his wife about his past indiscretions, and in the process lets slip that he has a secret about Humphrey's seemingly faultless past: an affair twenty-five years earlier with the village post mistress, Audrey Cuttle (Irene Handl), resulting in the birth of an illegitimate son. With a little prompting from Alfred, Audrey Cuttle is soon on his doorstep, birth certificate in hand, demanding hard cash in turn for her silence.

In adversity, the two fathers become the best of friends and, donning drag, Alfred soon has matters in control. By the closing reel, Audrey is revealed as a fraud, Fred and Cherrie are married and Humphrey has hung up his solicitor's robes and is running a bookmaking business with his former foe.

Background: Based on the 1948 popular West End stage play, it proved to be too naughty for the British censors and much of the film was left on the cutting-room floor. Audrey's part as the hotel receptionist, already small, all but disappeared. As one of the film's 'wild oats', her part was considered too risqué for British audiences. Her cheeky grin, flirtatious manner and line, 'Hotel Regency, Good Morning... Who? ... Mr Gilbey? ... Oh Hello Alfred', bracketed by Alfred's 'Listen Honey' and 'Goodbye My Sweet,' and interspersed with his lewd cackle, are all that remains of Alfred's extramarital friendship at the Regency Hotel.

Themes: **The Fashion:** Behind the hotel desk, Audrey wears a simple black dress with a wide white-collar, her hair swept up and little gold earrings. This is the image used on the video's sleeve, despite her thirty-second appearance.

The Older Man: The plot implies that the twenty-two year old Audrey is one of the many mistresses of Alfred Gilbey, played by Stanley Holloway. The next time they would appear together on-screen, Holloway would be playing Hepburn's father in *My Fair Lady*.

The Verdict: On its release, the film was a flop. *Picturegoer* (23 June 1951) described it thus: 'Undeniably successful on the stage, it has lost most of its unblushing zest and humour in transit and reaches us as a tired little weakling of a comedy with all the venerable clichés intact.'

The tired and dated theatricality of the piece does not translate well to the screen. The cast does not gel well together. The more theatrical actors (Hare, Lorne and Pearce) overplay their scenes, whilst the more realistic performances of Stanley Holloway and dare I say it, the young Audrey Hepburn, inject a sense of fun so lacking elsewhere.

Audrey Hepburn's thirty-seconds screen appearance and Stanley Holloway in drag are all that *One Wild Oat* has to offer. This slight and dated film would have been lost forever were it not Audrey's first English-speaking film role. 1/5

Laughter In Paradise (1951)

Cast: Alastair Sim (Deniston Russell), Fay Compton (Agnes Russell), George Cole (Herbert Russell), Guy Middleton (Simon Russell), Hugh Griffith (Henry Russell), John Laurie (Gordon Webb), Veronica Hurst (Joan Webb), A E Matthews (Sir Charles Robson), Joyce Grenfell (Elizabeth Robson), Anthony Steel (Roger Godfrey), Beatrice Campbell (Lucille Grayson), Eleanor Summerfield (Sheila Wilcott), Ronald Adam (Mr Wagstaffe), Audrey Hepburn (Cigarette Girl), Michael Pertwee (Stewart).

Crew: Produced and directed: Mario Zampi. Written by Michael Pertwee and Jack Davies. Cinematography: William McLeod. Music: Stanley Black. Edited: Giulio Zampi. Art Direction: Ivan King. Filmed in England. UK. 93 minutes.

Story: Henry Russell (Hugh Griffith) dies laughing at one of his own practical jokes. Has the world seen the last of his cruel pranks? No. His relatives, eager to get their hands on the booty, find themselves the unwitting butts of his one last practical joke. To gain their allotted £50,000, they each have to perform a task at odds with their character.

Agnes Russell (Fay Compton), his cruel and superior spinster sister, has to be a maid for one month without resigning or being fired.

13

Herbert Russell (George Cole), a timid and nervous bank clerk, has to hold up his own bank, and not be caught or overpowered for two minutes.

Simon Russell (Guy Middleton), the smooth-talking cad, has to marry within the week the first unmarried woman he talks to.

Deniston Russell (Alastair Sim), the author of salacious penny dreadfuls, has to commit a crime and spend twenty-eight days in prison.

The terms of the will cannot be disclosed to anyone outside the room, and as each potential recipient sets off, they little realise by fulfilling these tasks, their lives will change forever.

As Simon spends the evening celebrating his good fortune in a night-club, he speaks to the unmarried cigarette girl (Audrey Hepburn). Taking care not to get involved with any gold-diggers, and being both a cad and fool, he tells this young girl he can't talk to women for a while, to which she retorts, 'Don't I count?'

Over the next month, the four stories are neatly interwoven as Deniston finds it increasingly difficult to get arrested but quite easy to get himself in trouble with his fiancée Elizabeth (Joyce Grenfell) and his secretary, Sheila (Eleanor Summerfield). Herbert, easily bullied by fellow bank clerk Stewart (Michael Pertwee), finally plucks up courage to pull the bank job only to find himself the hero of the hour. Agnes spends a month with the wicked and tight-fisted Gordon Webb (John Laurie) and his young daughter Joan (Veronica Hurst). Not only does she manage to convince Joan to elope with the private detective her father hired to find out what Agnes was up to, but melts both her own and the miserly Mr Webb's heart in the meantime. Simon, only too confident that he can pull off the task by marrying an independently wealthy woman rather than one of his usual frivolous dates, finds himself tricked into marrying his butler's penniless niece.

With two of the four failing to complete their tasks, Agnes and Herbert both find love, strength and happiness they never thought existed. Deniston succeeds and spends a month in prison, but realises who he really loves and what he can achieve with the love of a good woman as a result. Simon, the one who thought his task simple, finds himself saddled with a gold-digger for a wife and no fortune as Henry Russell just had to have the last laugh - there is no money.

Background: Audrey Hepburn was dancing in the chorus of the West End stage production of *Sauce Piquante* when producer/director Mario Zampi spotted her and offered her a small part in *Laughter In Paradise*. Despite only having two scenes and a couple of lines, it propelled the young Audrey onto the front cover of March 1951's *Film Review*. Casting scouts for the upcoming *Young Wives' Tale* saw an early print of *Laughter In Paradise* and offered her a more substantial role in their movie.

Themes: **The Fashion:** Audrey looks beguiling in her 'cigarette girl' get-up of black satin dress, white bowed hair and her tray of cigarettes. She looks radiantly happy and at home in the glamorous night-club and on her first front cover.

The Older Man: Guy Middleton was twenty-three years older than Audrey Hepburn. They would both appear in *Young Wives' Tale*, in which he pursues the slightly maturer Joan Greenwood, who was eight years older than Audrey.

Trivia: Michael Pertwee, who co-wrote the screenplay with Jack Davies, plays the obnoxious bank clerk, Stewart, forever putting Herbert Russell in his place. He is also Jon (Dr Who) Pertwee's brother.

The film was remade in 1972 as *Some Will, Some Won't*.

The Verdict: Once again, Audrey had the tremendous luck of appearing with an all-star cast. *Laughter In Paradise* is a great, fun film. Alastair Sim and George Cole steal the picture and are ably supported by a host of popular character actors: Joyce Grenfell as Sim's army officer fiancée, as usual, was allowed to write her own part, John Laurie as Fay Compton's cantankerous love interest, and Hugh Griffith (a popular stage actor of the day, whom Audrey would work with again in *How To Steal A Million*) in the small but pivotal role of the ultimate practical joker, Henry Russell.

The four tales are neatly woven with each character's transformation, from greedy hanger-on to independence, cleverly structured. A comedy with a moral ending.

Audrey's performance as the cigarette girl who successfully manages to lure Simon from his vow not to speak to women, aptly shows the magic way Audrey manages to both light up the screen and steal a scene from her earliest opportunity. 4/5

Young Wives' Tale (1951)

Cast: Joan Greenwood (Sabina Pennant), Nigel Patrick (Rodney Pennant), Derek Farr (Bruce Banning), Helen Cherry (Mary Banning), Guy Middleton (Victor Manifold), Athene Seyler (Nanny Gallop), Audrey Hepburn (Eve Lester).

Crew: Director: Henry Cass. Producer: Victor Skutetzky. Written by Ann Buraby from the play by Ronald Jeans. Music: Philip Green. Art Direction: Terence Verity. Cinematography: Erwin Hillier. Edited: E Jarvis. Filmed in England. UK. 79 minutes.

Story: A film about the post-war housing shortage sounds like a strange concept for a comedy, but it is the ideal setting for the slapstick bedroom farce antics that pepper the film.

One house: lots of people. Mary (Helen Cherry), Bruce (Derek Farr) and their daughter Elizabeth live in a big London house, but because of the housing shortage, they are forced to share it with another couple - Sabina (Joan Greenwood), Rodney (Nigel Patrick) and their son Valentine. Also living there is Eve (Audrey Hepburn), a young typist who believes that every man is after her, but who is secretly obsessed with Rodney. To make matters worse, they also have to find space and a never-ending procession of nannies who are unable to cope with Valentine's raucous behaviour. Mary, a busy executive who spends more time in the office than at home, takes matters into her own hands to hunt down a new nanny. In an effort to ensure she stays, she tells her both children are Sabina's.

Chaos follows when Sabina - a resting actress - tries to run the house and simultaneously fend off the raffish black marketeer Victor (Guy Middleton). Alone one evening, she successfully escapes Victor's clutches only to be passionately comforted by Bruce. Nanny (Athene Seyler), popping in to ask whether they'd like some cocoa, makes the assumption that Sabina and Bruce are married, however, Rodney has no such delusions when he walks in a little later and still finds them at it. Storming off to his club, Rodney leaves Bruce and Sabina to face Mary alone, but she is so keen to keep nanny, she insists they carry on the pretence. Bruce returns the next morning and seeks solace in the arms of the young and inexperienced Eve, who admits that she has had no doomed love affair as she had implied and that unlike Sabina, will darn his socks.

However, all's well that ends well; the confusion, the bedroom farce sequence complete with smashing windows and falling downstairs, ends with all couples living happily ever after.

Background: Like *Laughter In Paradise*, British studio Associated British were financing the film. Victor Skutetzky, the film's producer, had seen some dailies from *Laughter In Paradise* and snapped Audrey up for her first substantial role. While the film was in production, the studio offered her a long-term contract. So, desperate for funds, Audrey signed with them. After completion, she was immediately loaned to Ealing Studios for *The Lavender Hill Mob*. Associated British would have made more money loaning out Audrey than she would have received. Michael Balcon at Ealing Studio bought out the contract after filming had completed on *The Secret People*.

Although the role of Eve was Audrey's largest to date, she had a rough time making this film. The film's director, Henry Cass, took an instant dislike to the young Audrey and made what should have been a wonderful experience simply unendurable. Later in her career, she still made reference to this film as being the only unhappy picture she'd ever made. Although Cass was so fierce that she ran from the set crying on several occasions, co-stars Nigel Patrick and Joan Greenwood remained a constant source of good cheer and protection among yet another cast of popular West End actors.

Whilst waiting around on set, Audrey whiled away the hours sculpting little models out of plasticine. Joan Greenwood commented that if she didn't make it as an actress, she could always become a sculptor.

Revenge must have been sweet for Audrey when Bosley Crowther, writing in the *New York Times* (12 November 1951), ranted that the film was as 'dismal [a film] as ever leaked from an uninspired brain', but advised audiences to watch out for 'that pretty Audrey Hepburn'. The film was re-released in 1954 after Audrey had achieved international acclaim with *Roman Holiday* and *Sabrina Fair*.

It was shortly after completing work on *Young Wives' Tale* that Audrey met James Hanson, her first serious beau.

Themes: **The Fashion:** Joan Greenwood had played the role of Sabina on-stage; one of the highlights for her when cast in the film was going to Paris and having her entire wardrobe designed by Christian Dior. It is only seeing Joan Greenwood and Audrey Hepburn in the same film that you realise how much of Joan's screen style and performance (except of course the former's wonderfully fruity voice!) the young Audrey must have absorbed during filming.

The Older Man: Although Eve is convinced that every man, young or old, is after her, she is only after the married Bruce Banning. The twenty-two-year-old Audrey continues her trend of being paired against an older man, as Derek Farr was seventeen years her senior.

The Verdict: A dated and stagy English comedy. Cass' decision to film most of the film in the confines of the house adds to the claustrophobic living conditions of the families, but does nothing to open out Ronald Jeans' West End play for the screen.

Audrey Hepburn's curious role of the young single secretary, who tries to convince those around her she has had a doomed love affair in her past, and that every man is chasing her, now seems very contrived. Nevertheless, she makes the best of what she's given in her half-dozen or so scenes. In no way a classic English comedy, but worth catching for Audrey's first significant role. 2/5

The Lavender Hill Mob (1951)

Cast: Alec Guinness (Holland), Stanley Holloway (Pendlebury), Sidney James (Lackery), Alfie Bass (Shorty), Marjorie Fielding (Mrs Chalk), John Gregson (Farrow), Edie Martin (Miss Evesham), Clive Morton (Sergeant), Ronald Adam (Turner), Sydney Tafler (Clayton), Audrey Hepburn (Chiquita).

Crew: Director: Charles Crichton. Producer: Michael Balcon. Screenplay: T E B Clarke. Cinematography: Douglas Slocombe. Music: Georges Auric. Editor: William Kellner. Filmed in England and Paris. UK. 82 minutes.

Story: The film opens in a sunny tropical clime...

Holland: 'Ah, Chiquita, Chiquita...'

The exquisite Chiquita walks behind Holland, nuzzles his neck.

'I hoped I'd see you…'

Pulling out a wad of money, he hands a roll of notes to Chiquita.

'You run along and get that little birthday present.'

Chiquita takes the money. 'Oh, but how sweet of you.' Kisses him and walks away.

Sergeant: 'You seem to have accomplished quite a lot in one year.'

Holland: 'One superb year.'

Cue flashback…

Holland (Alec Guinness), the mild-mannered bank clerk, has just days to go before his retirement. With that comes the burning desire to spend his retirement, not in grungy Lavender Hill, but somewhere far more superior and sunny - South America for instance. His job requires him to escort his bank's gold bullion as it is transferred from the branch to head office everyday. Everyday he fantasises about robbing the van of its precious cargo of gold bars. Sadly, his fantasy always ends with the practical problem of how to melt down the bars. That is, until Pendlebury (Stanley Holloway), a designer and manufacturer of tawdry holiday souvenirs, moves into the same boarding house.

They soon hit upon a plan. They'll steal the gold bars, melt them down, mould them into souvenirs of the Eiffel Tower, and ship them over to Europe. Once there, they would melt them down again, sell the gold and live out their twilight years in Rio.

Initially, all goes according to plan; they 'recruit' two sidekicks (Sidney James and Alfie Bass) and steal the gold bars. Holland goes unsuspected and is given a leave of absence, which he uses to assist in the transformation of the bars into towers. The goodies are shipped to Paris with Pendlebury and Holland in hot pursuit eager to get their hands on the lolly. All now goes horribly wrong, leaving Pendlebury and Holland involved in a high-speed chase down the Eiffel Tower staircase in pursuit of a gang of schoolgirls who have mistakenly been sold the souvenirs made of real gold. The chase leads them back to England, where Pendlebury falls into the arms of the police. Holland gets away with a dozen statues, which allows him a year of his dream life - with the lovely Chiquita (Audrey Hepburn) - in a sunny tropical clime.

Background: Despite her considerably larger speaking role in *Young Wives' Tale*, Audrey took a step back to appear as nothing more than a glamorous walk-on in this Ealing comedy. However, it is a much superior production. Director Charles Crichton's reputation and the chance to share the screen with Alec Guinness would have lured the young Audrey to this project.

In just one day on set, her work there was done, but her vision stayed with Guinness who was so impressed with Audrey's look and presence that he introduced her to the film director Mervyn LeRoy. LeRoy was at the time looking for a young actress to play Lygia in his production of *Quo Vadis*. Audrey did screen and costume tests but was eventually considered too young and inexperienced. The part went to Deborah Kerr, ten years her senior.

Themes: **The Fashion:** Again, beautifully dressed with a slight hint of the exotic: white tailored suit with black gloves, belt and handbag. A pearl necklace and matching earrings complete the outfit.

The Older Man: Surprisingly, compared with her previous co-stars, Alec Guinness is only fifteen years older than Audrey Hepburn. This is also the first of Audrey's many roles as the 'kept' woman.

The Verdict: One of the most enduring Ealing comedies, which combines equal amounts of villainy and comedy that make this, along with *Kind Hearts And Coronets*, *The Ladykillers* and *Hue And Cry*, such timeless masterpieces. Stanley Holloway, Alec Guinness and Sid James are all on top form, but is it a great example of an Audrey Hepburn film? Well, no. She looks beautiful but blink and you'll miss her role of Chiquita. Despite being such a small part, it would have looked good on her CV and as she often said, it meant that she could always claim to have acted with Alec Guinness. 5/5

The Secret People (1952)

Cast: Valentina Cortese (Maria Brentano), Audrey Hepburn (Nora), Serge Reggiani (Louis), Michael Allan (Rodd), John Field (Fedor Luki), Angela Fouldes (Nora as a child), Charles Goldner (Anselmo).

Crew: Director: Thorold Dickinson. Producer: Sidney Cole. Screenplay: Thorold Dickinson and Wolfgang Wilhelm. Based on a story by Thorold Dickinson and Joyce Cary. Cinematography: Gordon Dines. Filmed in England. UK. 98 minutes.

Story: A thriller set in pre-Second World War London sees two sisters, Maria (Valentina Cortese) and Nora (Audrey Hepburn), struggling to find peace in England following their escape from Europe. They had to leave an unknown European country after their father, a pacifist, became the target of a political assassination. Despite a new start, a few years pass and their past catches up with them. When Louis (Serge Reggiani), Maria's former fiancé, turns up, violence and tyranny surrounds them once again. Louis is now the leader of a group of ruthless saboteurs involved in a plot to assassinate a German dignitary. Maria abandons her father's political ideals and becomes a violent revolutionary, fighting alongside Louis. Nora, now a teenager and aspiring ballerina, is flattered by the handsome Louis who draws her into his sinister world. Once Maria realises the danger she has put Nora in, Maria finally turns on her compatriots and becomes a police informer in order to protect her sister.

Background: Audrey was cast principally for her ballet experience, but the small, pivotal role had many echoes of her own experiences - playing the heroine's sister, she is a dancer who is traumatised by the memories of a bomb explosion where many people where killed. Audrey's own experiences of living in Occupied Arnhem and her training with the Rambert Ballet Company made this a perfect transitional film for her. It was her first drama and through it she showed more acting ability than she had previously displayed. The shoot was hard work, as she had to spend much of the film in scantily clad ballet costumes, in freezing cold conditions at the famous (but very run-down) Bedford Theatre in London's Camden Town which was doubling for Dublin Opera House. Rehearsals and filming of the ballet sequences were completed over nine days. Only four minutes of footage appears in the final cut.

The Secret People had been in development for four years. Initially, Associated British were financing the project but became scared of the film's subject matter and, considering it too political, too intellectual, too downbeat, pulled the plug. Michael Balcon at Ealing was looking for more serious films as a way of increasing the studio's respectability - fearing that their stable of lightweight comedies would adversely pigeon-hole the studios. In hindsight, he couldn't have been more wrong. It is the comedies, *The Ladykillers, Kind Hearts And Coronets, Passport To Pimlico* et al., that have maintained an enduring presence in the heart of British cinemagoers. Their attempts at tackling serious subject matters have been assigned to the top shelves.

The production office for *The Secret People* was next to the sets for *The Lavender Hill Mob*. Lindsay Anderson, who was working on the film, recalls the ambitious Audrey popping into the office to enquire if there were any roles for her. Simultaneously, director Thorold Dickinson had spotted Audrey in the chorus of *Sauce Piquante* and had already made a note of her striking looks and personality. He thought that she'd be perfect for Nora, but was worried by her height when compared to the film's lead, Valentina Cortese, playing the older sister. Valentina took an instant liking to Audrey and between them, they devised a way of fooling Dickinson. Audrey did the screen test with bare feet and Valentina walked on tiptoe.

The Verdict: Upon release, the film was not a success, either critically or commercially, and has slid into oblivion. It occasionally turns up at the NFT. When it last appeared, Alexander Walker described Audrey's performance thus: '… her naturalness and simplicity, the guileless innocence that was her professional hallmark, show up radiantly - even with nothing to do she stays alert, poised, like a bird ready to flit off its branch.' Shooting began in February 1951, but it wasn't released until the following February, by which point Audrey had already starred with tremendous success on Broadway in *Gigi* and had already completed filming *Roman Holiday*. The film was poorly received in England and was not released in America for several years, by which point Audrey was a major Hollywood star and Oscar winner, and the film's limited release could cause her no harm now. Audiences were a bit surprised by her limited screen time.

Monte Carlo Baby
Nous Irons A Monte Carlo (1952)

Cast: Audrey Hepburn (Linda Farrell), Jules Munshin (Antoine), Russell Collins (Max), John van Dreelen (Rudy Walter), Michelle Farmer (Jacqueline), Philippe Lemaire (Philippe), Ray Ventura (as himself).

Crew: Director: Jean Boyer and Lester Fuller. Written by Jean Boyer, Alex Joffe and Lester Fuller. Producer: Ray Ventura. Filmed in France. France/UK. 79 minutes.

Story: In both French and English, *Monte Carlo Baby/Nous Irons A Monte Carlo* pretty much boils down to a series of skits and big band performances linked with a slight storyline. Linda Farrell (Audrey Hepburn) is an internationally famous French movie star. When an epidemic of measles closes a nursery, her son is mistakenly given to the custody of travelling musician, Max (Russell Collins). She and her estranged husband Rudy (John van Dreelen), a concert pianist, have to chase all over the Riviera searching for the missing squawker.

Background: Filming began on location in Monte Carlo at the end of May 1951, the day after she'd finished work on *The Secret People*. After *The Secret People*, Associated British's *Monte Carlo Baby* may appear to have been a retrograde step.

The story goes that Audrey felt that if she was to play a French movie star, she should have a more adventurous look. She visited her friend, Nick Dana, who quick as a flash, started snipping her long dark hair until she was left with the very modern gamine haircut that was to become her trademark, and copied the world over.

Monte Carlo Baby was filmed simultaneously in French and English. The film was released in France and England in 1952. It received a limited 'art house' release in America in 1954 after Audrey had become a star. Audiences were again confused that the star of *Roman Holiday* and *Sabrina Fair* had such a small part. As the film is now long forgotten, along with most of the cast, reference books now imply that Audrey Hepburn was the film's star. In reality, it was another bit-part as Audrey only appears in twelve minutes of the finished film.

Audrey had been initially reluctant to accept the role in this silly comedy, so she sought the advice of her *Secret People* co-star, Valentina Cortese, who encouraged her to go as it may lead to something better. Spoken like a psychic, it was whilst filming in the lobby of the Hotel de Paris that Audrey caught the attention of the novelist Colette. Colette had sold the rights of her novel *Gigi* to Broadway producer Gilbert Miller, but had inserted a casting approval clause for the lead role into the contract. Colette was immediately sure that Audrey was right for the part, but Miller took some convincing.

Themes: **The Fashion:** For the first time, Audrey got to wear a designer dress, designed by Christian Dior. As an added perk, Audrey would get to keep it.

Trivia: Jean Boyer was a prolific French director of his day. His next film would be *Crazy For Love* (1952), which made a star of Brigitte Bardot.

Michelle Farmer, who played Jacqueline, was the daughter of Gloria Swanson.

The Verdict: The film was not well received in either language or any country. The *New York Times* review in May 1954 described it thus: '...as witless a film exercise as ever was spewed from an ingenious camera. She [Audrey] made the film before she became one [a film star] in reality. It is rather astonishing how she stands out in that seared desert of mediocrity.'

3. Starring … Audrey Hepburn

Roman Holiday (1953)

Cast: Gregory Peck (Joe Bradley), Audrey Hepburn (Princess Ann, aka Anya Smith), Eddie Albert (Irving Radovich), Hartley Power (Mr Hennessy), Paola Carlini (Mario Delani), Harcourt Williams (Ambassador).

Crew: Director: William Wyler. Producer: William Wyler. Written by Dalton Trumbo [but credited to Ian McLellan Hunter]. Cinematographer: Franz F Planer and Henri Alekan. Filmed in Rome. US. 118 minutes.

Story: Princess Ann (Audrey Hepburn) is on a goodwill tour of Europe. Everything is going well until she reaches Rome. There, overtired, overworked and bored with all the 'wholesome' activities she has to endure, she escapes from her palace bedroom window and heads for the bright lights of Rome's café life.

Through another window we stumble across two American journalists, Joe Bradley (Gregory Peck) and Irving Radovich (Eddie Albert), successfully losing all their money in a game of cards. Joe leaves with only a few lira left, and like a knight in shining armour, comes across our sleeping princess.

Believing her to be drunk, he tries to get her home in a taxi but when she tells him to take her to the palace, he believes her so far gone that he takes her back to his place. The next morning, they both oversleep and both miss an important engagement: Princess Ann's press conference. Joe visits his editor and tries to bluff his way, but is caught short when his editor shows him a rival's paper stating that Princess Ann is unwell. He takes one look at the photo of Her Royal Highness and dashes home with a commission that, for an exclusive interview he'll get $250, for her views on clothes, $1,000 and 'for the works', $5,000.

Ann is his ticket home and with the aid of Irving's cigarette-lighter camera, they concoct a plan to tail the princess and later join her for her twenty-four-hour 'Roman holiday'.

New shoes, ice cream, a haircut, her first cigarette, getting chased by the police, being arrested, a date with a barber, visiting the Mouth of Truth, going dancing and becoming embroiled in a fight are all squashed into a day's fun and frolics, secretly captured on film by Irving. However, as the day progresses, Joe becomes rapidly reluctant to 'kiss and sell' as he and Ann begin to fall in love.

Background: Frank Capra had been seeking finance for this film for four years. With no sources imminent, he sold the project to William Wyler. Had Capra found the cash, it would have been *Roman Holiday* starring Cary Grant and Elizabeth Taylor.

With Wyler on-board, he sent the script to Gregory Peck, his first choice for the role of Joe. Meanwhile, the studio wanted Cary Grant and sent him a script.

Grant turned it down, so they agreed to allow Wyler to pursue Peck for the role. Peck, having read the script, also turned it down, saying that the film belonged to the princess, not the reporter. Wyler, craftily appealing to Peck's renowned lack of egotism, said, 'You surprise me … If you didn't like the story, okay, but because somebody else's part is a little better than yours … that's no reason to turn down a film. I didn't think you were the kind of actor who measures the size of the roles.' His tactic worked. With a marquee name on-board, Wyler was free to choose an unknown actress for the princess. His first choice was Jean Simmons, but Simmons, under contract to Howard Hughes, was unavailable and too expensive. Wyler, in London en route to Rome, was introduced to several young actresses, one of whom was Audrey. Screen tests followed, parts offered and problems reared their heads. Audrey was already contracted to appear in *Gigi* on Broadway. Wyler, assuming that *Gigi* would only run a month, signed her anyway for a salary of $12,500. Paramount was placated. If she did well in New York, they'd have a Broadway star in the film. If she didn't do well, what had they lost? One month turned into six as Audrey became the toast of Broadway.

Shooting was postponed, but eventually, when the cast and crew were assembled in Rome in June 1952, shooting began. It was a long and demanding schedule that was not completed until October. It was early on in the shoot that Gregory Peck made an important call to Hollywood, one that not many stars of his stature would make. He phoned his agent to demand that his lone above-the-title credit be amended to a shared billing with Audrey Hepburn. His reason? Audrey was stealing the show, and he would look mighty foolish come Oscar day when she wins Best Actress in a film where her credit was 'And Introducing Audrey Hepburn'. With the credits changed, the film opened at the Radio City Music Hall in August 1953 to resounding critical and commercial success. Audrey Hepburn was regarded as an overnight sensation, and Peck as a wonderful leading man in a comedy. As for Peck's prediction that Audrey would be an Oscar winner, well he was correct. The following year she was nominated for her first of five nominations. By the March, she was clutching her first Oscar to sit alongside her The New York Film Critics' Award and her Tony Award for Best Actress in her Broadway success, *Gigi*. She had arrived.

Themes: **The Transformation:** The overprotected princess yearns for adventure. On the streets of Rome she finds not only excitement, but transforms from a girl to a woman. She sneaks out of her bedroom with long hair, schoolgirl clothes, sensible shoes and the urge to rebel. Twenty-four hours later, when she sneaks back in, she has her hair cut and is wearing her outfit in a far more sophisticated way and, instead of flat sensible shoes, she is wearing strappy sandals. But more importantly, she now understands what her role is and makes the mature decision to abandon romance for duty and honour.

The Euphoric Moment: Princess Ann's twenty-four hours in Rome are full of euphoric moments, all of which are illicitly captured by Irving on his minicamera. Eating her 'first ice cream', such a simple pleasure that 'commoners' would take for granted, but for her, it is her first experience of freedom. However, the key euphoric moment has to be Joe's and Ann's ride on a Vespa around Rome. In the early 1950s, the Vespa was new and sexy, and Hollywood wanted to exploit this - it was shown to be a romantic way to see a city. In a 1990s BBC TV documentary on the Vespa, the Mayor of Rome said that, even now, people feel like Gregory Peck and Audrey Hepburn when they ride their Vespas around Rome.

The Older Man: Cary Grant was initially offered the role of Joe Bradley but turned it down believing that the twenty-five-year age gap would jeopardise his career. Gregory Peck's (only thirteen years older) only concern once he'd met Audrey was that she would steal the film.

The Fashion: Despite Audrey's reputation for fashion, she only wears a handful of costumes (all designed by Edith Head, Paramount's studio Fashion Chief) for this film: a sumptuous ball-gown at the film's opening ball, her frumpy nightdress, her transformation into a city gal when on the streets of Rome, Bradley's pyjamas and a severe formal suit for the film's final press conference.

The film opens at a formal ball where Princess Ann has to shake hands with a long line of dignitaries. But our focus is not on her gorgeous gown, but what is happening under the petticoats: foot acrobatics. Tired feet are her downfall and she happily slips off her shoes to massage her feet. However, on sitting down, like Cinderella, she loses one of her shoes on the steps.

After the ball, she petulantly remarks that she hates all her night-gowns and underwear, and what she'd really like to do is to sleep in pyjamas - just the top half at that. When she stays over at Joe's, she gets her wish and he lends her the top half of his pyjamas.

For her night-time escapade, Ann wears a simple white blouse and fawn skirt. However, by simply rolling up the sleeves, unbuttoning the top buttons and wrapping a scarf around her neck, she is transformed from a formal 'schoolgirl' to a vibrant young woman about town. On her own for the first time, and with 1,000 lire in her pocket, she steps out onto Rome's city streets and finds herself in a market. The first thing she buys is a pair of comfortable strappy (and sexy) sandals.

For the last scene, she is dressed in white, but not a wedding dress, a formal suit. And instead of embracing her lover, she smiles and, with a tear in her eye, leaves the room.

Trivia: The front cover of the 9 September 1953 issue of *Time* magazine featured a portrait of Audrey Hepburn painted by Boris Chaliapin. This was the first and last time that they'd dedicated a front cover to an unknown film actress.

The release of *Roman Holiday* saw Japan's immediate love affair with Audrey Hepburn. The Japanese film poster had a huge portrait shot of Audrey and a tiny image of Gregory Peck. Throughout her life, Audrey only appeared in one television campaign and that was in 1971 for a Tokyo wig manufacturer. This is ironic, as it was Audrey's gamine haircut that swept across the hair salons of Japan in 1953.

This was Audrey's first 'Hollywood' film, yet she had never seen the studios for whom she was under contract, nor even been to Hollywood.

It was at the film's London premiere that Audrey met Mel Ferrer.

At the time it was assumed that Princess Ann's adventures were based on those of Princess Margaret.

The film's screenwriter, Dalton Trumbo, was on the infamous Hollywood blacklist by the time the film was made and so the screenplay was credited to Ian McLellan Hunter.

The Verdict: Probably one of the most exquisitely stunning romantic comedies of all time. As a debut American film, Audrey could not have asked for a more perfect role, co-star or director. The dialogue is witty and the cinematography, for the most part on location in Rome, looks impressive and adds a certain charm and sunlight that could not have been captured on a backlot in Hollywood.

It is a bitter-sweet fairy tale as Princess Ann tells her 'prince' they have to part otherwise she will, 'turn back into a pumpkin and ride away in my glass slipper.' In the film's final frames, Joe turns back to see where Ann has been ushered out. He is waiting for the happy ending. We are waiting for the happy ending - the one where Princess Ann runs across the palace reception hall and falls into Joe's arms - but it doesn't come. The moral? Life is not a fairy tale. A perfect film. 5/5

Sabrina Fair (US: Sabrina) (1954)

Cast: Humphrey Bogart (Linus Larrabee), Audrey Hepburn (Sabrina Fairchild), William Holden (David Larrabee), Walter Hampden (Walter Larrabee), John Williams (Thomas Fairchild), Martha Hyer (Elizabeth Tyson).

Crew: Director: Billy Wilder. Producer: Billy Wilder. Screenplay: Billy Wilder, Samuel Taylor and Ernest Lehmann from Taylor's play. Cinematography: Charles Lang Jr. Editor: Arthur Schmidt. Costume: Edith Head and Hubert de Givenchy. Filmed on location on Long Island, New York. US. 114 minutes.

Story: The Larrabees and the Fairchilds are two families living on Long Island. The Larrabees are wealthy and successful. Walter Larrabee (Walter Hampden) and his elder son Linus (Humphrey Bogart), are hard-working whilst David (William Holden), the younger son, is something of a cad and playboy.

Thomas Fairchild (John Williams) is the family chauffeur living above the garage with his daughter Sabrina (Audrey Hepburn).

The scrawny and plain Sabrina has been nursing a one-way crush on David Larrabee for some time. In an effort to separate his daughter from her adolescent fantasy, Thomas sends her off to Paris for two years to learn to cook. Whilst there, she is transformed from a caterpillar into a butterfly.

On her return to the Larrabee mansion in Long Island, David is besotted by her and wonders why he never noticed the lovely Sabrina before. But his timing couldn't have been worse, as he has just become engaged to Elizabeth Tyson (Martha Hyer), the sugar cane heiress, and Linus is using this marriage to cement a multi-million-dollar deal with Tyson's father.

With just ten days to David and Elizabeth's wedding, Linus has to sabotage the burgeoning romance between Sabrina and David and reunite him with Elizabeth before the wedding day. But little does he realise that his hard heart and level head can be so easily turned.

Background: Sabrina Fair is an adaptation of Samuel Taylor's Broadway play, which had starred Joseph Cotten and Margaret Sullavan. Audrey Hepburn had first come across it during her run on Broadway in *Gigi* and had persuaded Paramount to buy it for her as a suitable vehicle after *Roman Holiday*. They agreed and so Audrey embarked on her second grown-up fairy tale for which she was paid the princely sum of $15,000 and was to receive second billing, sandwiched between Humphrey Bogart (earning $30,000) and William Holden (also $15,000).

The playwright, Samuel Taylor, had been hired by Paramount to work with Billy Wilder in adapting his play for the screen. But he was so appalled by the huge sections Wilder was removing that he stormed off, and Ernest Lehmann was hired to complete the job. By then, filming was due to begin and Wilder and Lehmann continued working on the script after each day's shooting. Actors would arrive and be given whole new scenes to learn. But this was the least of the behind-the-scenes problems. Bogart had only reluctantly agreed to be in the film and spent his time between shots endlessly drinking bottles of whisky. He goaded and mimicked Hepburn and, when Wilder tried to intervene, he became the butt of his crude imitations.

The film was shot over nine weeks on location in Glen Cove, Long Island, on the estate belonging to Paramount's Chairman, Barney Balaban.

Audrey didn't have a chance to go to Paris whilst filming. The Paris scenes were all filmed in a studio. She did, however, go before filming to select her wardrobe. It was felt that as the character was to acquire a Paris wardrobe, so should Audrey Hepburn - and much to Edith Head's dismay, who had hoped of creating the post-Paris costumes - the job went to Parisian couturier Hubert de Givenchy.

27

The off-screen romance between Holden and Hepburn created a tense atmosphere on set. Holden was married, devoutly Catholic and was unable to have any children. For Hepburn, who longed to be a mother, this was the final blow and so ended their relationship.

Themes: **The Transformation:** Unlike *Roman Holiday*'s two-day transformation from child to woman, here it took two years. On both occasions, the cutting-off of long, unruly hair and a change in clothes and outlook are essential. Although it is never made explicit, I fear our Sabrina may have been a kept woman whilst in Paris for those couple of years. She is quickly taken under the wing of a wealthy aristocratic Baron when she fails to master the simple elements of fine cuisine. He arranges for a wardrobe full of evening gowns, the radical new haircut and trips to the opera. When she left America she was a child; she returned a woman.

The Euphoric Moment: Sabrina's most euphoric moment is when she returns from Paris and arrives at the train station. She is the most sophisticated person there and is stranded. David picks her up but does not recognise her. She teases him the entire journey home. At the end, he invites her to the Larrabee party she has longed to attend since a child. On her arrival, her charade is shattered by Linus who recognises her immediately.

The Older Man: Cary Grant, originally offered the role of Linus Larrabee, turned it down, once again convinced that the age gap (twenty-five years) was too great. The role finally went to Humphrey Bogart (thirty years older) with his cancer making him look considerably older. Tension between the young Hepburn and Bogart was further aggravated by Hepburn's affair with her other co-star, William Holden (eleven years older), whom Bogart loathed.

The Fashion: Edith Head, Paramount Fashion Chief, designed all Hepburn's pre-Paris transformation outfits. She had initially expected to design all Audrey's costumes as she had done for *Roman Holiday*. In her autobiography, *The Dress Doctor*, she wrote, 'The director broke my heart by suggesting that, while the "chauffeur's daughter" was in Paris, she actually buy a Paris suit.' She ended up buying much more than a suit. Hubert de Givenchy designed all the clothes worn during the scenes set in Paris (once she falls in league with the Baron) and for all the clothes worn on her return to Long Island. This film was the start of a relationship between Givenchy and Hepburn, which lasted until she died. Audrey looks stunning, especially in her Givenchy gowns. Her first entrance at the Larabees' party easily equals that of Eliza's arrival at the Embassy Ball in *My Fair Lady* for sheer head-turning appeal.

Trivia: Despite constant comments on the age gap (thirty years) between Audrey Hepburn and Humphrey Bogart, it is worth remembering that at this time, Humphrey Bogart was happily married to Lauren Bacall - twenty-five years his junior.

The Verdict: Billy Wilder, one of the greatest directors working in Hollywood during its Golden Age, had his work cut out for him: convincing us that Sabrina would choose Linus over David. And he very nearly pulls it off. This is one of those movies where, despite the odd moment here or there, which in the hands of another director could make you feel a little queasy, it is a pleasure to watch.

The locations: filming on location in Long Island, New York, adds to the film's authenticity and the excesses of the Larabees' lifestyle is mirrored by the immaculate design of the home and gardens.

The screenplay: a crackling screenplay which tackles tricky issues of life, love, money and class in an intelligent and witty way.

However, it is Audrey's performance that makes this film 'sublime'. Considering that this was only her second leading role, she handles herself with great aplomb.

Like many of Wilder's 'comedies', *Sabrina Fair* is tinged with bitter-sweet cruelty where both the performers and their characters are laid bare, making them far more sophisticated than any number of other romantic comedies being made at this time. 4/5

War And Peace (1956)

Cast: Audrey Hepburn (Natasha Rostov), Henry Fonda (Pierre Bezukhov), Mel Ferrer (Prince Andrei Bolkonsky), Vittorio Gassman (Anatole), Herbert Lom (Napoleon), Jeremy Brett (Nicholas), Oskar Homolka (General Kutuzov), Anita Ekberg (Helene), Milly Vitale (Lisa).

Crew: Director: King Vidor. Based on the novel by Count Leo Tolstoy. Written by Bridget Boland. Cinematography: Jack Cardiff. Filmed in Italy (Rome) and Yugoslavia. Italy and US. 205 minutes.

Story: A big screen adaptation of Tolstoy's epic tale of three families caught up in the Napoleonic Wars from 1805 to 1812.

The Families

The Rostov Family: Natasha (Audrey Hepburn) is a bright young tomboy (despite first seen wearing a pretty yellow dress and swinging ponytail) who bemoans the fact that it is her brother, Nicholas (Jeremy Brett), that gets to go off to war and have all the fun whilst she has to stay at home.

The Bosuloff Family: One of her family's closest friends is Pierre (Henry Fonda), the illegitimate son of Count Bosuloff. On his deathbed, the Count begs the Tsar to give Pierre the title and lands. Pierre's evil cousin Helene (Anita Ekberg), who only moments before treated him like dirt, is suddenly batting her eyes and giving him come-hither looks. He soon finds himself seduced by the duplicitous Helene. They marry but she spends more time fussing over her new hats and shoes than she does her husband.

The Bolkonsky Family: His best friend is Prince Andrei (Mel Ferrer), who is married to the dull and pregnant Lisa (Milly Vitale). Their marriage has long been over and, when she dies giving birth, it is to Pierre that he seeks support.

The Romance

So Andrei and Pierre head off into the country for a few days' peace and quiet. It is there that Andrei meets the bright, beautiful and considerably younger Natasha whilst out riding. They all spend the weekend at Pierre's country estate where Andrei overhears Natasha discussing him favourably. Over the next few months they fall in love and plan to marry. He joins the army and they decide to postpone their wedding until he gets back - if they really love each other, a year isn't that long. But while he's away, Natasha catches the eye of Helene's brother, Anatole (Vittorio Gassman), and he plans to seduce the young and inexperienced Natasha. His flattering remarks and eagle-eyed stares wear her down and she finally succumbs and is prepared to throw everything away for this grand passion.

The War

Russia is at war with Napoleon (Herbert Lom). Andrei and Nicholas are both in the thick of it. Pierre reluctantly enters into the fray but soon finds himself a prisoner. The Russian Army retreat and Moscow falls. Napoleon is triumphant but gets bored as what's the point of taking over Moscow when there are no Russians left to surrender to him?

Natasha arranges to help the wounded escape Moscow and finds out that Andrei is one of those saved, and even in his delirious final days, he forgives her. Further tragedy strikes when she discovers that Nicholas has also died.

Napoleon, bored and fed up, goes home to France and the Rostov family return to their home to Moscow to rebuild their life.

Background: War And Peace was filmed in Rome and Yugoslavia on a budget of $6 million.

Audrey's salary was $350,000, plus a generous weekly expense account and bonuses if filming went over the scheduled twelve weeks. Despite this being only her third American feature film, Audrey was now receiving top billing, even over more well-established co-stars such as Henry Fonda and Herbert Lom.

Audrey was given the power to hire key technical personnel. The film's British cinematographer, Jack Cardiff, was hired at Audrey's request. He obviously enjoyed working with her as he said, 'When Audrey walks on set, the camera will automatically follow her.'

But all was not a bed of roses as, not for the first time, gossip-mongers reported that Ferrer had only been cast in the film on the back of Audrey's fame and that he was causing chaos on set by making demands for himself and his new wife. These have been vigorously disputed by the film's respected director, King Vidor.

Themes: **The Transformation:** Natasha is again a young 'chit of a girl' at the beginning of the film - it isn't until she gains Andrei's affections that she begins to change, and she is finally transformed through Anatole's wrongdoing of her. Her disillusionment has made her stronger; has made her a woman. This is reflected in the change in the colours of her costumes as they change from the yellows and pastels of youth to the grey colour of mourning.

The Euphoric Moment: At her first ball she dances with Prince Andrei. Not only is it her first ball, but she also wears her first full-length gown. Having attracted the attention of a prince, they dance together. Vidor has implemented the use of the internal monologue to suggest their growing feelings for each other; 'If she looks back on the next turn - I'll marry her.' She does.

The Older Man: Mel Ferrer was Audrey's leading man both on and off the screen. On-screen, this gap is shown by him being already married, widowed and endowed with a world-weary fatalism. Off-screen, at twelve years her senior, she looked to him as a mentor who could protect her and help in guiding her career.

Henry Fonda, at fifty, was cast as Pierre, Natasha's most enduring love.

The Fashion: The costumes designed by Marie de Matteis are used to symbolise the stages in Natasha's development from girl to woman. The yellow frocks of girlhood are replaced by drab grey and black dresses of mourning. After Andrei's death and the departure of the French, her family return to Moscow. Once there, she begins organising and looking after her shattered and broken family. She is seen wearing a long sophisticated red dress showing her rebirth and another stage in her development.

Packing her clothes to escape Moscow, she gives some to her maid. When she comes across the dress, which she wore to her first ball, for a flickering second she is transported back there - in a flashback - and she is happy once again, if only briefly.

Trivia: Filmed during the summer in the Cinecitta studios in Rome, several tonnes of artificial snow had to be made for the film.

Jeremy Brett was to appear as Audrey's admirer, Freddie Eynesford-Hill, in *My Fair Lady*.

The screenwriter, Bridget Boland, was a leading West End playwright of the day.

The Verdict: Although she is largely absent for the first half-hour, Audrey Hepburn's role as Natasha becomes the film's core and she manages to convey the changing emotions as she transforms from a girl to a woman with great skill. But as to the film itself, it is long (3¼ hours but feels longer) and one that never quite breaks out of being a worthy adaptation of Tolstoy's epic. It never feels like a passionate and vibrant film in its own right.

The large-scale battle sequences are impressively staged and shot as one would expect from King Vidor. There are key sequences that work well, but overall this, like many films of the period, is an overlong and turgid film, with the producer trying to fit the whole of Tolstoy's epic in without taking into account the visual medium of film. 2/5

Funny Face (1957)

Cast: Audrey Hepburn (Jo Stockton), Fred Astaire (Dick Avery), Kay Thompson (Maggie Prescott), Robert Flemyng (Paul Duval), Dovima (Marion), Michel Auclair (Professor Emile Flostre).

Crew: Director: Stanley Donen. Screenplay: Leonard Gershe. Music: George Gershwin. Lyrics: Ira Gershwin. Choreography: Hermes Pan. Filmed in Paris and Paramount Studios, Hollywood. US. 103 minutes.

Story: Celebrated fashion photographer Dick Avery (Fred Astaire) is hired by Maggie (Kay Thompson), the editor of *Quality* magazine, to photograph clothes for women who are not interested in clothes. Down in Greenwich Village he spies the perfect 'intellectual' location - a book shop, specialising in philosophy, run by the dull and drab Jo Stockton (Audrey Hepburn). After the shoot, the crew departs leaving the shop in a mess, but Dick's intuition tells him that there is something special about this 'funny-faced' girl and stays behind to tidy up.

Later, when the magazine is looking for a woman to embody the *Quality* woman - Dick champions Jo. Having succeeded in convincing his boss, he now only has to convince the deeply philosophical Jo that fashion and modelling and a trip to Paris isn't all bad. With the lure of Parisian intellectuals and beatnik cafes, she finally agrees to go.

Once there, Dick photographs Jo all over Paris in a series of stunning gowns. The final shoot of her in a wedding dress forces the couple to recognise the shift in their relationship. But Jo still has her heart set on meeting Professor Emile Flostre (Michel Auclair). On the night of the big fashion show, she finally succeeds when he invites her to one of his intimate and exclusive salons. She jumps at the chance, leaving all thoughts of Dick and the fashion show behind. Dick and Maggie, in one of the film's most surreal musical numbers, pose as beatniks and gatecrash the party where they sing a song entitled 'Clap Yo' Hands', which sends up the whole movement. Jo brusquely sends Dick away, but when she realises that Flostre is only interested in her to make love to, not talk to, she hits him over the head and runs off. She runs back to the fashion show in search of Dick, but it is too late as he's on his way back to New York. But will they get together for the final reel, kiss, make up and sing 'S'wonderful'? Of course, this is the perfect romantic musical comedy.

Background: Based on Fred Astaire and his sister Adele's Broadway and West End hit of the 1920s, *Funny Face* was drastically revised and updated to the 1950s as a vehicle for Fred Astaire who, following the break-up of his long partnership with Ginger Rogers, had been keen to avoid a regular partner and was once again on the lookout for a new young co-star. The initial plan was to hire Carol Haney - who'd received acclaim for her Broadway role in the *Pyjama Game*. But she wasn't considered a big enough name and the project was put on hold. Meanwhile, Audrey, keen to utilise her dancing skills, championed herself for the role. With Mel acting as negotiator, he fought for a deal which paid her $150,000 plus a generous living allowance - generous enough to rent a suite of rooms at the Paris Ritz. She also got to keep all her Givenchy gowns. Deals were struck between MGM (who owned the script) and Paramount (who owned Audrey and Fred). A $1 million deal was done and they were ready to roll. The film's final budget was $3 million.

After a period of shooting at Paramount Studios in Hollywood, the production moved to Paris in April 1956. It was an exceptionally rainy April and Audrey reminisced that it was just her luck that when she got to fulfil her childhood dream of dancing with Fred Astaire, she fell over in the mud!

At the time, critical response to the film was mixed. They loved the book, the songs, the dance numbers, the cast - particularly Audrey (who had worked incredibly hard to make the most of her singing voice) and Fred Astaire. However, they felt that he was now a little too old to play the romantic lead.

Themes: **The Transformation:** Jo is an intellectual and therefore drab and bookish, wears glasses, has her hair tied back and wears shapeless dresses, thick black tights and flat shoes. She spends her time with her head in a book. On her arrival in Paris, rather than attending the 'Salon of Duval' (a Parisian designer based largely on Givenchy himself), Jo heads to an existential night-club where she meets beatniks and intellectuals, but not her great hero Professor Emile Flostre (the genius behind empathaticalism, her favoured philosophical theory). When she finally shows up at Duval's, an army of hairdressers and make-up artists transform this funny-faced 'lowly worm' into a 'bird of paradise', far exceeding their butterfly hopes. But it takes some time to get her head out of his books and into the clouds.

The Euphoric Moment: There is a montage sequence of Dick taking Jo's photographs. They start stiffly and formally and as the couple get to know each other, begin to fall in love. The photos become more and more stunning as Jo takes the initiative and strikes her own poses. In one session, she doesn't tell him what she's going to do. She just shouts out for him to start clicking, comes out from behind a statue wearing a stunning red dress, and runs down the large flight of steps of the Louvre. With her flowing red scarf flying behind her and a look of pure happiness across her face, she finally embraces life and love.

The Older Man: Despite being one of Hepburn's oldest leading men (thirty years her senior - the same age gap as Humphrey Bogart), Astaire manages to carry off the role with his usual panache and style, ably supported by the film's witty script. Audrey said, 'I remember the first time we met: he was wearing a yellow shirt, grey flannels, a red scarf knotted around his waist instead of a belt, and the famous feet were clad in soft moccasins and pink socks. He was also wearing that irrepressible smile. One look at this most debonair, elegant and distinguished of legends and I could feel myself turn to solid lead, while my heart sank into my two left feet. Then suddenly I felt a hand around my waist and with inimitable grace and lightness, Fred literally swept me off my feet. I experienced the thrill that all women at some point in their lives have dreamed of - to dance, just once, with Fred Astaire.'

The Fashion: As the film is set in the 'exclusive fashion salons of Paris', expect lots of glamorous gowns and outfits. Givenchy designed Audrey's Paris wardrobe, all of which are knock-outs: from the white pedal-pushers and bare midriff top she wears whilst fishing on the banks of the Seine to the stunning flame-red chiffon she wears whilst running down the steps of the Louvre.

But Edith Head's contributions must not be underestimated. She designed all other costumes including Audrey's sack-dress over a black sweater, thick black tights and clumpy shoes as really worn by all the best 'serious-minded' students of the day on both sides of the Atlantic. Head is also aware of the importance of costume for comic purposes. When magazine editor Maggie Prescott decides that everyone should 'think pink', all costumes and sets are transformed to pink, except of course Maggie who remains (as she does throughout the entire film) in a grey business suit. And we mustn't forget Astaire's costumes - the short white raincoat set a male fashion for years to come.

Trivia: Dick Avery (Fred Astaire) is based on the photographer Richard Avedon, whose stills are used in the fashion spreads.

Maggie (Kay Thompson) is based on *Harper's Bazaar's* editor, Carmel Snow.

Kay Thompson was the author of an extraordinarily popular series of novels about *Eloise*, a precocious pre-*Lolita* six-year-old living in the Plaza, New York.

The Verdict: 'This wonderful dramatic star is a revelation in her first musical comedy' so screams the film's original theatrical trailer. And she is. Singing all her own songs, Audrey carries off her first musical comedy with grace and humour. The plot is witty and fresh with huge sideswipes at the fashion industry and fashion photography - with which Audrey has become synonymous. Also under attack is the burgeoning beatnik generation - Fred Astaire's and Kay Thompson's costumes and subsequent dance number when they gatecrash an 'empathaticalist' party is a hoot. As is Thompson's 'Think Pink' (*Legally Blonde* can't even compete with pinkness of this sequence) and the gorgeous 'S'wonderful' number at the film's finale. The package is perfect and, as always, Givenchy's gowns enhance both Hepburn's and Paris' beauty. 5/5

Love In The Afternoon (1957)

Cast: Gary Cooper (Frank Flannagan), Audrey Hepburn (Ariane Chevasse), Maurice Chevalier (Claude Chevasse), Van Donde (Michel), John McGiver (Monsieur X), Lise Bourdin (Madame X).

Crew: Director: Billy Wilder. Written by Claude Anet and I A L Diamond. Cinematographer: William C Mellor. Filmed in Paris, France. US. 130 minutes.

Story: This is the tale of a girl with no experience who turns the table on the most experienced man in the world.

Frank Flannagan (Gary Cooper) is the greatest connoisseur of women.

Claude Chevasse (Maurice Chevalier) is the most famous love detective in Paris.

Ariane Chevasse (Audrey Hepburn) is delightfully, completely innocent.

So claims the film's trailer.

The setting is Paris and Claude Chevasse is a private eye hired by a cuckolded husband (John McGiver) to gather evidence on the American millionaire play-boy Frank Flannagan. Claude's daughter Ariane overhears the husband threaten to kill Frank for his late-night shenanigans in his hotel room and heads off to divert disaster.

Having been successfully rescued by Ariane, Frank begins to seduce his new 'captive' and being both young and impressionable, and intrigued by her father's most profitable quarry, becomes entranced and agrees to see him again, but not without having done a little homework. Breaking into her father's office, she reads the file on 'The World's Greatest Lothario', about the divorces he's caused, the scandal, and the attempted suicides of his 'victims'. Shocked by the true nature of the cad, she determines only to meet him to tell him that she can't come. But it is too late. His well-worn routine of the Mariachi band, champagne and moody lighting soon kicks in and she's seduced. But as he is always between planes, that evening he flies back to New York and she returns home to mope.

Over the next year, she reads about his escapades in the press and begins to date Michel (Van Donde), a fellow music student. Then one night she bumps into Frank at a concert and they begin to see each other once again. Using all the information she has amassed on him, she plays him at his own game and makes him believe that she is as experienced as he is. Making up a mythical and racy past compiled from her father's case histories, her list of conquests grows longer and longer, and Frank becomes more and more jealous. So jealous that when he meets up with the cuckolded husband, he is receptive to the idea of hiring a private eye and takes him up on his suggestion that Claude is the man for the job.

Frank tells Claude about his mystery girl, and Claude deduces that the mystery girl is none other than his own daughter and that as she loves him, he should get out of town and fast. But will Frank be able to leave Ariane behind? Or has the man who can't be hooked, finally found his match?

Background: Based on Claude Anet's novel *Ariane*, which was first filmed in 1931 in Germany with Elizabeth Bergner in the lead, Wilder and I A L Diamond (in their first collaboration), worked together to update the plot and mould it for Audrey's unique girl/woman quality. As with *Sabrina Fair* and *Roman Holiday*, there are references to Audrey's appearance (as being unattractive), and here Frank Flannagan calls her 'Thin Girl' throughout as she refuses to tell him her name.

Gary Cooper was suffering from recurrent hernias and duodenal ulcers when filming began and looked much older than his fifty-six years. Wilder was concerned that his gaunt and ageing features would be too difficult for audiences to overcome and shot his scenes through gauze filters, upstaging him and keeping him in the shadows. This itself brings about another set of problems in the finished film. In his attempts to keep Cooper's face hidden, we never really get to know Flannagan, as his character and personality are removed. We are left with no real reason why this young girl would be so besotted by him - except that the part is played by Cooper.

Themes: **The Transformation:** At the beginning of the film, she wears frumpy clothes and has hair in a very unattractive style, but by the end of the film, she is wearing far more glamorous clothes. Her attitude changes alongside the physical transformation, and her relationship with a (much) older man blossoms.

The Euphoric Moment: Spoiler coming up: When she sees him off at the station, she runs alongside the train, until he reaches down and swoops her up in a great moment of euphoria.

The Older Man: Ariane Chevasse is supposed to be a seventeen-year-old music student (Audrey was twenty-eight). Rumours suggest there was some tension on set between Maurice Chevalier and Gary Cooper. With Chevalier only three years older than fifty-six-year-old Cooper, he was upset that he was cast as the father and Cooper as the lover. But as Cooper was twenty-eight years older than Audrey - both were old enough to be her father. And for the third time, Cary Grant turned down the offer of acting opposite Audrey Hepburn - would they ever get together on-screen?

The Fashion: The little black dress or simple Capri pants and top - all clothes suitable for a girl of her age and social background, but I fear the Givenchy price-tag might have been a little bit of a student's budget.

In a daringly provocative way for the day, she uses the chain from her cello case as a sexy anklet for one of her dates with Flannagan - such chains were at the time only worn in real life by 'women of low virtue'.

Trivia: Billy Wilder's wife (also an Audrey) appears briefly as Flannagan's date at the opera.

The voice-over at the end of the film, telling us that they were soon married, was added following negative audience reactions at seeing the wholesome and child-like Audrey mixed up in a sleazy affair with a man who seemed to be old enough to be her father.

The Verdict: There are those who would claim that Cooper was far too old for the part. Many, therefore, find the implications of the central romance a little troublesome. But the age gap only heightens the comedic notion that this innocent chit of a thing manages to run rings around a man who has been around the block a few times. In the hands of another director, the subject matter could have become rather seedy. Wilder's direction is so stylish and witty that he can get away with it. Remember, one of his first big hits was *The Major And The Minor* (1942), where a fully formed Ginger Rogers poses as a thirteen-year-old girl to get a reduced train fare only to attract the attentions of an Army Major (Ray Milland).

Love In The Afternoon is a much underrated romantic comedy. The film's second half is especially well written and acted when the tables are turned on Flannagan and the 'hit and run lover' finds himself flattened by the beguiling Ariane. The scene where he repeatedly plays back her dictated list of lovers while the Mariachi band play in the background is a particularly fine moment. 3½/5

The Nun's Story (1959)

Cast: Audrey Hepburn (Sister Luke/Gabrielle van der Mal), Peter Finch (Dr Fortunati), Edith Evans (Mother Emmanuel), Peggy Ashcroft (Mother Mathilde), Dorothy Alison (Sister Aurelie), Ludovice Bonhomme (Bishop).

Crew: Director: Fred Zinnemann. Screenplay: Robert Anderson. Based on the novel by Kathryn Hulme. Filmed in Belgium, Italy and the Belgian Congo (later Zaire, now the Democratic Republic of the Congo). US. 149 minutes.

Story: This adaptation of Kathryn Hulme's factually based best-selling novel (set in the late 1930s) tells the story of Gabrielle (Audrey Hepburn), who becomes a nun in the hope that she will be sent to the Congo to work as a nurse among the natives. Her father, a well-known surgeon, supports her choice. For six months she has to live with other postulants in almost prison-like conditions where there is a rule of silence, which is a hard reality for the young Gabrielle. After this initial period, the postulants become novices and, in a 'wedding ceremony', their hair is cut and they have to give up all their worldly possessions and marry Christ. Now known as Sister Luke (after St Luke who was a doctor), she devotes herself chiefly to helping in the hospital, her devotion to God seeming secondary. Her patients tell her that she makes a beautiful nun as she has all the qualities needed: discipline, obedience, self-will, charity and humility. But the senior nuns are not so sure. When she attends the School for Tropical Medicine, she excels and seems sure to pass the exams. But a senior nun tells her she must deliberately fail the exam so another sister can go to the Congo instead and that this would demonstrate her humility. Unable to do this, she is punished and sent to work with the most dangerous cases in a mental sanatorium, hoping that this would teach her to be obedient. She is finally sent to work in the Congo.

Once there, Sister Aurelie (Dorothy Alison) breaks the news that she won't be working in the native hospital but in the 'white' hospital, assisting Dr Fortunati (Peter Finch) and supervising the nurses. She makes great headway and is praised by all those with whom she comes into contact; she works hard but neglects her prayers and finally succumbs to a form of tuberculosis.

Dr Fortunati wants her to stay with him so he can treat her, but advises that the main problem is not the illness but her commitment to being a nun. Sister Luke is ordered to escort a sick patient back to Belgium. There she is ordered to rest and renew her spiritual life.

With Europe on the brink of war and her future path unclear, her mind wanders to the Congo and Dr Fortunati. But her services are needed at home and she is posted as a surgery sister on the Dutch border. With bombs falling around them, they carry out their duties to the utmost. When the town becomes occupied, she becomes involved in the underground movement, which is against the wishes of the convent. Her father's death makes her question her life and she decides to leave the order.

Background: Because of Audrey's wartime background, when she had worked for the Dutch resistance, she was keen to play Kathryn Hulme's heroine, Gabrielle, a dedicated missionary nurse. She breaks her vows in order to work with the Belgian Resistance movement during the Second World War. The character of Gabrielle was an amalgam of the true-life experiences of Kathryn Hulme and Marie-Louise Habets, who had met at a United Nations refugee camp in Germany after the Second World War.

Both were actively involved in the film, with Marie-Louise Habets spending considerable time with Audrey, instructing her in the life of a nun and the handling of surgical instruments.

It had been Zinnemann's plan to film at the Sisters of Charity Convent in Belgium, but the Bishop of Bruges refused permission. The film's production designer, Alexander Trauner, then had to recreate the entire convent and chapel at Rome's Cinecitta Studios. No convent in Belgium would allow Audrey to visit for research purposes, but she did, however, spend a few days at a French convent.

The cast and crew also went to the real locations, travelling to them by boat from Stanleyville (now Kisangani). Filming began in January 1958 and lasted three months with food and provisions being flown in twice weekly from Belgium. Little would they know that in less than a year, this area would be subject to a violent revolution, leaving many of the real nuns dead.

In a sequence that mirrors what Audrey herself would face many times in later life, Sister Luke finally arrives in the Congo where she is welcomed by the faces of hundreds of waving and smiling black children.

Although filming for *The Nun's Story* was completed before her next project, *Green Mansions,* had began, it opened a couple of months after the release and critical savaging of the latter. In contrast, *The Nun's Story* received a rapturous response from the critics, a healthy box office return and six Academy Award nominations, including Best Picture, Director and Actress, which thankfully helped wipe out all memory of *Green Mansions*.

Themes: **The Transformation:** This film is all about transformations as Gabrielle grows up in a complex environment. Initially, she has to absorb the realities of life in a convent. Gone is the relative freedom she enjoyed at home, helping her father in his lab. She has to devote herself to God and is not free to make her own decisions. Despite her rebelliousness within that environment, she finally fulfils her dream of working in the Congo. There, she once again enjoys a certain level of freedom and is able to make decisions that are not necessarily in line with her order. She also feels an uneasy pleasure at spending time with the charismatic Dr Fortunati and this takes her away from her marriage to Jesus, as the doctor makes her feel like a woman, not a nun. Her final transformation is when she decides to leave the order. When she finishes removing her habit and changing into the clothes provided, she presses a button and the door to the outside world is opened. She walks through and down a cobbled road to a new life.

The Euphoric Moment: A nun's life doesn't lend itself well to moments of euphoria. But Sister Luke is delighted and feels a great sense of personal self-worth when she walks into her compartment on the boat back to Belgium from the Congo and finds it full of flowers and gifts from the natives.

The Older Man: Peter Finch plays Dr Fortunati, the man who makes Sister Luke question her commitment to religion. Not only is he considerably older, he is a surgeon like her father who she had to give up day-to-day contact with in order to fulfil her dream of becoming a nurse and working in the Congo.

Peter Finch's reputation as a hell-raiser, drinker and womaniser complemented his role as the charming and slightly dangerous doctor. Although there is no explicit romance between the two, there is an implicit attraction between the doctor and the nun.

The Fashion: Although it suits many British actresses, only Audrey could make a habit look quite so alluring even though it was not designed by Givenchy. The tight-fitting wimple framing her face makes it look more luminescent than ever.

Trivia: In one of the film's prop photographs of Gabrielle and her fiancé, the young man posing with her is Audrey's half-brother Ian.

The Verdict: A truly remarkable performance by Audrey Hepburn, displaying an emotional depth not previously seen. This is a film that does not rely on her clothes, looks or personality in order to generate attraction and audience involvement. It is a dark and sombre film; the extensive sections of the film set in the convent offer a fascinating look at the life of a young novice, which are contrasted with the bright open scenes set in the Congo. This is Audrey's film - she carried the entire weight of the film on her shoulders and bears the task remarkably, aided by the completely different style of acting from those two great dames of British theatre - Edith Evans and Peggy Ashcroft. 4/5

Green Mansions (1959)

Cast: Audrey Hepburn (Rima), Anthony Perkins (Abel), Lee J Cobb (Nuflo), Sessue Hayakawal (Runi), Henry Silva (Kua-Ko), Nehemiah Persoff (Don Panta).

Crew: Director: Mel Ferrer. Written by William Henry Hudson and Dorothy Kingsley. Based on W H Hudson's novel. Filmed in British Guiana, Venezuela, Columbia and Hollywood. US. 100 minutes.

Story: It's the turn of the century (nineteenth to twentieth that is) and Abel (Anthony Perkins) is an impetuous young man who is trying to escape the revolution and heads for the Interior. But his erratic behaviour soon frightens off his guides and he finds himself alone, with only a small bundle of possessions and being attacked by a leopard. Rescued by a gang of Indians, he is taken back to their village where he tells them his life story. Abel is after hidden gold, and spying an ornate necklace around Chief Runi's (Sessue Hayakawal) neck, surmises that he is the man to get to know better.

Believing that the source of gold is to be in the forest which Runi has forbidden all Indians from going into, he heads off there. He finds not gold, but a strange warbling whistling sound that leads him to a lagoon where he sees the reflection of a young beautiful woman (Audrey Hepburn). He returns to the village and tells them of his adventures and of the mysterious girl. They in turn tell him of the legend of the forest and of Runi's eldest son who was killed by this strange girl who they call 'The Daughter of the Deedee'. As he came back alive, they believe that he must posses magic powers and instruct him to return and enact their revenge by killing her.

He does go back to the forest, not to kill her, but to warn the Daughter of Deedee. But before getting the opportunity, he is bitten by a snake. He wakes up two days later in a hut, where he finds that he is being looked after by an old man, Nuflo (Lee J Cobb), and his granddaughter Rima, the mysterious young woman. As she nurses him back to health, he discovers that she has no memory of her childhood, but this does not prevent them from falling in love.

Abel's loyalties are now torn between his love for Rima, his desire for the gold and his gratitude towards the Indians who first saved his life. He returns to the village where he tries to tell the Indians that Rima is just a girl and that she possesses no sinister powers, but they don't believe him and tie him up. Managing to escape, he runs to Rima and Nuflo and they go on the run together heading towards Rio Lama - the village where Rima's mother had lived. Their journey back to Rio Lama brings back memories for both Nuflo and Rima. Nuflo, unable to keep the truth to himself, tells Abel that he is not Rima's grandfather but a murderer and thief who stole the Rio Lama's precious gold and killed all the villagers, including Rima's mother. Rima overhears his confession and falls into a fever. With their roles reversed, Abel now nurses her back to health. Full of remorse, Nuflo leaves in the night and makes his way back to the hut where he finds the Indians waiting and, as he digs up the stolen Rio Lama gold, the Indians set the hut on fire. Rima, now concerned for Nuflo, leaves the sleeping Abel and returns to the destroyed hut where she finds Nuflo's dying body among the ruins. Listening to his dying words, she doesn't initially hear the Indians approaching; running in fear of her life she climbs a tree. The fire-obsessed Indians set light to the base of the tree and it quickly spreads upwards with Rima trapped at the top, who can do nothing but cry for help.

Abel is on the way to rescue her. At the lagoon where he first saw Rima, he now confronts Kua-Ko (Henry Silva), the Chief's son, who proudly tells him of his victory over the 'evil spirit' Rima and the old man. They fight and Kua-Ko is killed. Abel goes in search of Rima and finds nothing but the blackened and destroyed tree. But where is Rima? How did she manage to escape? Does she indeed possess magical powers?

Background: Based on W H Hudson's popular adventure romance, attempts at filming it had been ongoing for some time. Initially bought by RKO as a Delores De Rio vehicle, it lay languishing there for eleven years before being sold to an independent producer, who in turn sold it to MGM. In 1953, Alan Jay Lerner had a stab at writing a screenplay, which was liked, and Vincente Minelli was brought on-board to direct Pier Angeli, but during pre-production the project was dropped. However, when Mel Ferrer approached MGM with Audrey on-board, the project was resurrected and noted Broadway playwright Dorothy Kingsley was hired to write the screenplay.

Whilst Audrey was in the Congo filming *The Nun's Story*, Ferrer travelled throughout South America, filming exterior footage. It was felt that after her gruelling filming schedule in Africa, Audrey wouldn't have been up to another extreme location shoot as had been originally intended and the remainder of the film was shot on the MGM backlot.

The film opened in the spring of 1959 and received a brutal set of reviews and box office results. Although salvation for Audrey would come a couple of months later when *The Nun's Story* opened to great reviews and six Academy Award nominations, it could have only rubbed salt into Ferrer's wounds.

Themes: **The Transformation:** Rima begins the film as a girl of the forest, one feared and hated by the Indians and, through the course of events, she becomes a woman who loves and is loved in return. She grows up not by letting go of her childhood but by finally learning the truth and accepting her 'grandfather' for the man he is, not who he once was.

Abel also undergoes a transformation caused by his love for Rima and his adventures in the rainforest. To begin with, he is a greedy and cowardly man: he came in anger, searching for gold to pay for the revenge of his father but finds love and somewhere to belong.

The Euphoric Moment: The film's strange metaphysical ending offers the film's only moment of joy. Rima has been killed by the Indians and as Abel grieves, he remembers the story of the hutta flower that blooms for only one day before vanishing and reappearing elsewhere. Rima, a child of the forest, is able to perform the same trick. Once reunited, they walk off into the sunrise.

The Older Man: This is the first time that Audrey was older than her leading man (by three years). With her husband behind the camera, possibly only one father figure was needed.

The Fashion: Despite having negotiated the Givenchy clause in her contract, it was deemed inappropriate for Audrey to wear *haute couture* in the rainforest, hence all costumes were designed by Dorothy Jeakins. Audrey Hepburn wears the same simple dress throughout the film, but varies her look with a number of different hairstyles.

Trivia: In 1959, Anthony Perkins was considered a hot, young, leading man. Little did anyone know that only a year later he would star in a film that would end his leading man status forever when he was cast as Norman Bates in Alfred Hitchcock's *Psycho*.

The Verdict: Not even Audrey Hepburn can rescue this dated and tiresome film. Beautiful landscapes and a good solid performance by Anthony Perkins help, but Audrey, now married and having had a miscarriage, seems a little uncomfortable playing the eternal waif. The role of Rima, the bird girl, offers none of the challenges she had so enjoyed in *The Nun's Story*. 1/5

The Unforgiven (1960)

Cast: Burt Lancaster (Ben Zachary), Audrey Hepburn (Rachel Zachary), Doug McClure (Andy Zachary), Audie Murphy (Cash Zachary), John Saxon (Johnny Portugal), Albert Salmi (Charlie Rawlins), Charles Bickford (Zeb Rawlins), Lillian Gish (Mattilda Zachary), Kipp Hamilton (Georgia Rawlins).

Crew: Director: John Huston. Written by Alan le May and Ben Maddow. Costumes designed by Dorothy Jeakins. Filmed in Mexico. US. 125 minutes.

Story: Not to be confused with Clint Eastwood's 1999 western of the same name, John Huston's *The Unforgiven* is set in a remote part of Texas after the Civil War. Audrey Hepburn plays Rachel, a fresh-faced, wild and spirited child. She constantly ignores her mother's pleas of order and routine in favour of cross-country bareback horse riding and hanging out with her three brothers, Ben (Burt Lancaster), Andy (Doug McClure) and Cash (Audie Murphy).

But Rachel is no ordinary young woman. She is a woman with a past. With the sudden arrival at their home of the mad old man and a posse of Indians who offer Ben four horses in exchange for Rachel, Ben is forced to question the truth about her and how she came to be found on their doorstep. The Zacharys are in the business of taming wild horses and are in partnership with the Rawlins family. But it is not just business that the two families have in mind. Charlie Rawlins (Albert Salmi) wants to marry Rachel, and his sister Georgia (Kipp Hamilton) wants to marry any of the Zachary boys but has set her heart on the eldest, Ben. Charlie, in an attempt to impress Rachel, goes up against an acknowledged untameable horse from which he is thrown, much to his chagrin and Rachel's delight. Charlie, jealous and uncomfortable, starts a fight that Ben breaks up, having come to the realisation that Rachel is no longer his baby sister but a desirable young woman.

Background: *The Unforgiven* was a big-budget western ($6 million), with Audrey picking up $200,000 for her role. It was to be a hard, hot shoot in Mexico. Audrey was pregnant again and used to the cooler environs of Switzerland. She suffered (along with the rest of the cast and crew) with the primitive living conditions - especially the winds blowing dust everywhere - just the sort of location to which Huston notoriously liked to subject his actors.

Dust was not the only thing flying through the air; insults were being hurled too. Lancaster (also one of the film's producers) and Huston were at loggerheads over the film's direction. Later in his career, Huston said that of all his films, this was his worst and wished he could disown it.

This was the first film in which Audrey had to ride and she was using a horse called Diabolo, which had once belonged to President Batista of Cuba. One day it threw her and she was rushed to hospital in Durango and then to Los Angeles where she spent three weeks recovering from four broken vertebrae in her back. Wearing a restrictive neck brace, she returned to Mexico to continue filming where, as always, she was a complete professional and threw herself into the role, continuing to work and ride. Despite her efforts to protect her unborn child, she once again had a miscarriage. Returning to Switzerland for rest and recuperation, she discovered that she was once again pregnant and taking no chances this time, turned down all offers of work until after the birth of her first child in July 1960.

Themes: **The Transformation:** It is only when other men on the ranch begin to notice that she is no longer a little girl that her older 'brother' Ben recognises she is a desirable woman. The look he gives her after he has to break up a fight that started over her gives her the courage to speak to him in a mature fashion and state that they can marry as they are not really kin.

The Euphoric Moment: Despite all the chaos (and death) that ensues at the film's dramatic shoot-out, Ben still finds time to propose to Rachel. At the end of the battle, and with the Zachary family reunited, a flock of birds flies overhead in formation, a metaphor for a better future in Wichita.

The Older Man: Burt Lancaster was sixteen years Audrey's senior.

The Fashion: Once again Audrey's costumes were deigned by Dorothy Jeakins: wide circle skirts and simple blouses, as becomes a girl living out in the West.

Trivia: Audie Murphy nearly drowned when his boat overturned on a lake whilst out fishing. He was rescued by photographer Inge Morath (who later married Arthur Miller) who saw the accident through her telephoto lens.

It cost $350,000 to build the Zachary family home; the cost to build the real thing in 1860 would have been about $150.

The Verdict: This was the second film in a row where Audrey Hepburn played an Indian girl rescued by one of the people who had murdered her real family and brought her up as their own family, only to find out the truth when she becomes of age - and this is a far superior film to Mel Ferrer's *Green Mansions*.

It is downbeat and moody but ravishing to look at with well-drawn performances from Hepburn as a young girl who slowly comes to realise that her whole life is a sham. Although this dry, dusty landscape is not the milieu with which we usually associate Audrey, she turns in a great performance as Rachel, a young woman coming to terms with her sexuality and true identity.

It is a slow-burn western, where Huston allows us to get to know the characters, explores their relationships and how events within the film shape their attitudes. Despite Huston's misgivings, it is a testament to his majestic vision and his strength in eliciting strong performances from all involved. 3½/5

Breakfast At Tiffany's (1961)

Cast: Audrey Hepburn (Holly Golightly/Lulamae Barnes), Patricia Neal (Liz), George Peppard (Paul Varjak/Fred), Buddy Ebsen (Doc Golightly), Mickey Rooney (Mr Yunioshi), Martin Balsam (O J Berman), Jose Luis De Villallonga (Jose), Alan Reed Sr (Tomato), John McGiver (Tiffany's Salesman).

Crew: Director: Blake Edwards. Written by George Axelrod based on Truman Capote's novel. Filmed in New York. US. 115 minutes.

Story: $50 every time she goes to the powder room. $100 for an hour's prison visit with the notorious mobster Tomato (Alan Reed Sr); this is how the beautiful Holly Golightly (Audrey Hepburn) earns her money in 1960s New York. When Paul (George Peppard), a struggling writer and toy boy (he gets a furnished apartment and $300 left on the bedside table) moves into the apartment upstairs, they find a common ground and growing affection for each other.

Liz (Patricia Neal), Paul's lover and financial sponsor, fears that she is being followed. But complications ensue when Paul challenges the man. It transpires that it was not Liz he was watching, but his wife - Lulamae (known to us as Holly Golightly). Doc (Buddy Ebsen) wants Holly to come home as her brother Fred is coming out of the army, and he wants them all to be a family together again. Holly convinces him that she could never return to the farm and be his Lulamae, and he finally agrees to annul their marriage.

Paul sells his first story. To celebrate, they spend time taking it in turns doing things they've never done before. Starting with champagne before breakfast - the day ends with Paul and Holly going to bed, but the next morning he wakes to find she's gone. Paul tries to break off his financial and romantic relationship with Liz but she just gives him $1,000 and a week off with pay. Tracking down Holly, he learns that she has agreed to marry a rich Brazilian businessman, Jose (Jose Luis De Villallonga).

She becomes 'divinely happy' for a short while until she is arrested by the narcotics squad for helping Tomato in his illegal trade by unwittingly passing messages to his gang on the outside. The front-page headlines frighten Jose off, but she decides to hot-trot it to Brazil with or without him. In a cab to the airport, Paul tries to stop her going by telling her that he loves her but she dismisses him. Can Paul stop Holly from leaving? Will the ring he found in a crackerjack box melt her heart? And what of her cat, Cat? Can she really leave New York and start a new life?

Background: Blake Edwards flew to Switzerland to persuade Audrey to play the part of Holly Golightly. Despite her concerns over Holly's morality and news that Truman Capote wanted Marilyn Monroe for the part, she finally succumbed to Blake's charm. In the autumn of 1960, she travelled with her husband and their three-month-old son to New York where they filmed on location in Manhattan.

Almost immediately she began to regret her decision. There were large crowds of onlookers at every street corner and she became concerned for Sean's safety. In addition, George Peppard, a graduate of Lee Strasberg's Actors' Studio, had been cast opposite her. She found his 'Method' School of Acting hard to adjust to - as a consequence she began to smoke heavily and lose even more weight.

Themes: **The Transformation:** There is no on-screen transformation here. Holly has already been remodelled: as O J Berman says, 'She's a phoney - it took one year to get rid of her hill-billy accent.' We only see the 'hill-billy' Holly (or Lulamae as she was then) in Doc's photos.

The Euphoric Moment: Paul sells a short story and he and Holly decide to spend the day celebrating by doing things they've never done before. Taking it in turns, they start the day with champagne before breakfast (a novel experience for Paul, not Holly!) followed by a walk in the morning (Holly), a trip to Tiffany's (Paul), to the library (Holly) and finally shoplifting from a 5 & 10 cent store (Paul). This montage sequence is shown as vignettes of delight culminating on their daring raid at the 5 & 10 cent store - they return home and spend the night together.

The Older Man: One leading man. One husband. Lots of lovers. For the first time, one of them is the same age (George Peppard). As the story requires, her husband is a much older man with a large brood of children. In this instance, Buddy Ebsen was twenty-one years her senior.

The Fashion: For the film's first half, she is seen wearing mainly black for social engagements but, when she decides to marry Jose, she changes to pink. She then redecorates her apartment (South American style) and starts to wear casual clothes, doesn't have her hair done and begins to put on weight and claims to be 'divinely happy'.

Trivia: Celebrity photographer, Howell Conant, was hired to take the publicity shots for the film. His assistant brought in his cat from home for some of the shots. Unfortunately, whilst Audrey was petting the said cat, it disgraced himself, ruining one of her Givenchy frocks.

Audrey's performance of Henry Mancini's song 'Moon River' was almost cut from the film, with producers wondering why Holly would be sitting on a fire escape singing to herself. The only recording of it is on the film's soundtrack.

The Verdict: Much of Capote's original novella had to be cleaned up to accommodate Audrey's concerns - there was no way she could have played the part as written by Capote. As such, the final film is a bit of a mishmash as Peppard is clearly shown as a toy boy to his brittle older mistress. As Holly Golightly, Hepburn walks that fine line between the good and bad girl, erring more towards a girl out for a good time rather than Capote's loose-moraled, bisexual call girl. However, most embarrassing to contemporary audiences is Mickey Rooney's turn as Holly's cantankerous upstairs neighbour, the Japanese

Mr Yunioshi - which doesn't walk the fine line of fun/racism, but rubs it out and circles it around him. But then that is probably due to Blake Edwards - his direction of comedy is often a trifle heavy-handed.

On the one hand, it is sad to see Truman Capote's thrilling and vibrant novella transformed in such a vapid way. On the other, it does capture the wonderfulness of Audrey Hepburn. She has been captured on celluloid in all her translucent glory. The small moments from this film will remain with you for always: eating a croissant for breakfast outside Tiffany's, sitting on the fire escape singing 'Moon River', setting a hat on fire with her long cigarette, and standing in the rain with Cat and Paul. 4/5

The Children's Hour
(aka The Loudest Whisper) (1961)

Cast: Audrey Hepburn (Karen Wright), Shirley Maclaine (Martha Dobie), James Garner (Doctor Joe Cardin), Miriam Hopkins (Mrs Lily Mortar), Fay Bainter (Mrs Amelia Tilford), Karen Balkin (Mary Tilford).

Crew: Director: William Wyler. Written by John Michael Hayes. Filmed in US. 107 minutes.

Story: The Wright-Dobie School for Girls is run by Karen Wright (Audrey Hepburn) and her friend Martha Dobie (Shirley Maclaine). Also living there is Martha's Aunt Lily (Miriam Hopkins).

They have a nice set-up: a small private school, where the majority of the girls are polite and helpful. But there is always a rotten apple and here it is the thoroughly horrid Mary (Karen Balkin) who is always stirring up trouble, bullying the other pupils and spying.

When the school finally breaks even and they make their first profit ($90), Martha wants to use it to buy clothes for Karen and it soon becomes clear that Martha is in love with Karen. But Karen is oblivious to her friend's infatuation, as she is busy being wooed by the handsome Doctor Joe Cardin (James Garner). However, there is tension between them as Karen won't marry him until the school is up and running. He sees this $90 breakthrough as all he needs to persuade her to marry him and she finally agrees to this at the end of the school's term.

Although Aunt Lily is exasperating, she is perceptive and senses Martha's hostility towards Karen and Joe's romance and confronts Martha, announcing that she is jealous. Two girls overhear and report back to the nasty Mary about this 'unnatural' friendship. It's only a matter of time before she passes on the gossip to her grandma, Mrs Tilford (Fay Bainter) - who goes to the school to try to unearth the truth. There she bumps into Aunt Lily who has just been banished from the school. In her clumsy way, she spills the beans about her argument with

Martha and her view of the 'friendship' between the two schoolmistresses. Mrs Tilford adds two and two and makes five, quickly pulling Mary out of school but not before stopping off to tell the news to as many mothers as possible. Gossip spreads with the wind and within twenty-four hours, the school is empty and Karen and Martha are left wondering what has happened as no explanations were given by any of the parents. Finally, they discover the reason for the sudden evacuation and confront Mrs Tilford, who happens to be Joe's aunt.

Joe remains loyal to Karen and Martha despite severing his family ties and being fired from his job at the hospital. Karen and Martha sue Mrs Tilford for slander but lose the case. They become virtual prisoners in the house as sightseers stop by. The situation becomes progressively worse and even the discovery that Mary made the whole story up does not end the tragic chain of circumstances she unwittingly began.

Background: After the epic *Ben Hur* (1959), director William Wyler was keen to develop a smaller, more intimate feature and dug out *These Three,* his 1936 version of Lillian Hellman's controversial stage play, *The Children's Hour.* Believing that the play's frank subject matter (lesbianism) would be more readily accepted in the 1960s than it was thirty years before, he thought he'd have another crack at it. Despite a more liberal decade of movie-making, there was still the issue of getting the script passed by the Production Code. This would only be considered if the word 'lesbian' was never uttered, only implied.

After *Breakfast At Tiffany's,* Audrey was once again concerned by the film's subject matter, but was flattered that William Wyler, who had directed her in her first screen Oscar-winning role, wanted her for the part. Her fears were confirmed when the film was universally panned on its release in March 1962.

Themes: **The Transformation:** The arc of the film's narrative is a transformation for Karen. At the beginning of the film she is a frail and passive cipher for the affections of Martha and Joe. But as events in the film develop she becomes stronger. It is she who says she and Martha must stand their ground and fight for their names to be cleared as they have done nothing wrong. She matures from being a naive young woman to one filled with bitterness and hardness.

The Euphoric Moment: Very few euphoric moments: the closest you get in this dark and depressing film is the film's final frame where she walks away with her head held high into an unknown future - but at least she walks away with dignity.

The Older Man: The gap is closing. James Garner is only one year older than Audrey!

The Fashion: No Givenchy here. Simple elegant clothes that befit a struggling, penniless schoolteacher.

Trivia: Miriam Hopkins, who plays Aunt Lily here, starred as Martha in the original screen version, *These Three* (1936), also directed by William Wyler.

The Verdict: Despite Wyler's attempts to modernise the play's themes, he wasn't brave enough. The result, therefore, is the heart and soul of the film has been cut, leaving a gaping hole where the play's genuine issues of lesbianism and morality have been hacked. What remains is a somewhat tired, dated and old-fashioned film. Wyler is revered as one of the Golden Age's greatest directors and had nurtured Audrey through her first Hollywood film to Oscar glory, but by 1962, films were beginning to change and *The Children's Hour* has more in common with his 1940s melodramas than a film made and released in the 1960s, where a new generation of film-makers and audiences were emerging.

Shirley Maclaine has the showier and trickier of the two roles as the closet lesbian, but Audrey retains a dignity and naiveté as the love interest for both Martha and Joe. Her androgynous figure adds to this. Overall the film is an uneven and plodding affair which fails to live up to Wyler's expectations. 2/5

Paris When It Sizzles (1964)

Cast: William Holden (Richard Benson), Audrey Hepburn (Gabrielle Simpson), Gregoire Aslan (Police Inspector Gilet), Raymond Bussieres (Gangster), Christian Duraleix (Maitre d'Hotel).

Crew: Director: Richard Quine. Written by Julien Duvivier and Henri Jeanson. Filmed in Paris, France. US. 110 minutes.

Story: Richard Benson (William Holden) is holed up in a hotel trying to write a script entitled *The Girl Who Stole The Eiffel Tower* for his impatient director (Noel Coward). With just one weekend to conceive and write the screenplay, he hires Gabrielle (Audrey Hepburn) to do the typing. As he dictates his bad, dull screenplay, we see it come to life with the parts played by Audrey Hepburn and William Holden. The film cuts between the growing relationship (aided by drink and witty dialogue) between Benson and Gabrielle in the hotel suite, and the adventures of the film within the film become more complex and cheesy. As the film reaches its climax, the identities between the real and the fantasy have become fused.

Background: After her unhappy time in Hollywood on *The Children's Hour*, Audrey jumped at the chance to make this light and frothy romantic comedy in Paris with Richard Quine directing. She felt that a summer in one of her favourite cities would restore her flagging spirits. However, it was not to be...

Problems were occurring both on and off set, largely caused by her co-star William Holden, who had been drinking heavily when they made *Sabrina Fair* nine years before and with whom she had had an affair, had continued drinking and nursing his crush on Audrey. Their reunion for this film proved to be troublesome and fuelled a pattern of erratic behaviour on Holden's part. Quine had tried to monitor his drinking by moving into an adjacent house but failed and had to witness a series of bizarre incidents beyond his control.

During the shoot, Audrey's Burgenstock home was burgled and her Oscar, and much of her underwear, was stolen. It transpired that a young fan stole the goodies and turned himself in, hoping he would get to meet Audrey at the trial. The Oscar was found in a nearby wood, but her underwear was never recovered. The fan would never get to meet his idol as she did not attend the trial. Audrey's son was with her in Paris but with Mel filming in Spain, she began to worry for her family's security and relocated to a heavily guarded chateau outside Paris.

Although filmed in the summer 1962, it was shelved for two years and finally released in 1964 after the success of her Paris set romantic thriller, *Charade*.

Themes: **The Older Man:** By 1964, William Holden was a sad shadow of his former glorious self - attempts to rekindle the on- and off-screen flame that they had once enjoyed fizzled rather than sizzled. Their eleven-year-age gap looks more obvious with Hepburn's radiance remaining, and his, dimmed by years of alcohol abuse.

The Fashion: Despite being a 'young lady from the typing bureau', she wafts around his apartment in a Givenchy wardrobe and perfume.

Trivia: Look out for Mel Ferrer playing Dr Jekyll and Mr Hyde at the Eiffel Tower costume party.

Noel Coward noted in his diary for 1 October 1962: 'Audrey H. is unquestionably the sweetest and most talented girl in the business.'

The film's first cinematographer was Claude Renoir (grandson of Jean Renoir). When Audrey viewed the first set of rushes, she disliked what she saw and arranged for Renoir to be replaced by Charles Lang.

The Verdict: The script is poor and the film's final conceit is that the film we have just seen, about a couple writing a film and of the fantasy sequences from the film they are writing, are both in fact films within *Paris When It Sizzles* - the film we have just seen is an overcomplicated and glib solution to a mess of a film. William Holden is no longer up to handling the light and frothy material. Audrey on the whole looks embarrassed. Even the parade of big-name stars (in cameo roles) including Noel Coward, Mel Ferrer, Tony Curtis and Marlene Dietrich can do nothing to relieve the tedium of the two central characterisations.
1/5

Charade (1963)

Cast: Cary Grant (Peter Joshua/Alexander Dyle/Adam Canfield/Brian Cruickshank), Audrey Hepburn (Regina 'Reggie' Lampert), Walter Matthau (Hamilton Bartholomew/Carson Dyle), James Coburn (Tex Panthollow), George Kennedy (Herman Scobie), Ned Glass (Gideon), Dominque Minot (Sylvie).

Crew: Director: Stanley Donen. Written by Peter Stone and Mare Behm. Filmed in Paris, France. US. 113 minutes.

Story: Regina 'Reggie' Lampert (Audrey Hepburn) is holidaying with her friend Sylvie (Dominque Minot) when she first flirts with a charismatic American, Peter Joshua (Cary Grant). Her skiing trip was designed to put some distance between her and secretive husband Charles. Little did she know how much distance, as on her return to Paris she discovers her apartment empty (and I mean completely empty) - all furniture, possessions and more tragically, her wardrobes of clothes have all disappeared, as has her husband. The police had been waiting for her return to take her to headquarters. There, she is confronted with the news that the husband she was about to divorce is dead. If that wasn't news enough, she discovers that he had been leading not a double life, but a quadruple one, when she is presented with four passports. To top it all, the quarter of a million dollars that he got from the sale of all their stuff is missing.

Into her life once again appears the dashing yank - Peter Joshua. She soon discovers that his appearance isn't quite as innocent as it at first seemed when Reggie finds herself pursued by three unsavoury men (James Coburn, George Kennedy and Ned Glass). She first encounters the men at her husband's funeral when they come to check that he really is dead. They are all intent on killing her and reclaiming the quarter of a million dollars they reckon her husband stole from them. The chase is on. Will Reggie find the money before the three thugs kill her? Who is this mysterious and charming Peter Joshua who always seems to be in the right place at the right time? And who is the secretive and sinister Bartholomew (Walter Matthau) who she is summoned to meet at the American Embassy? And will Audrey Hepburn and Cary Grant finally get to kiss? The twists and turns continue until the moonlit showdown outside the Paris Opera House.

Background: At last, it was a long time coming, but finally Cary Grant and Audrey Hepburn appeared in the same film. The miracle maker behind the pairing was *Funny Face* director, Stanley Donen. Filming began in Paris in October 1962, mere weeks after her miserable experience on *Paris When It Sizzles*, but in contrast, the shoot was a happy one despite the cold autumn and winter.

It was released in December 1963 to enthusiastic reviews and became a box office hit. As Audrey's contract with Universal gave her a percentage of the profits, this must have been the icing on the cake.

Themes: **The Euphoric Moment:** Despite being a thriller, at its core it is really a romantic comedy. You have two attractive people and we delight in following them on their journey as they fall in love (and in this case, dispose of a few bodies along the way). There is no real surprise as to how the romantic element of the film is going to end, but when it finally comes, it's a real delight.

Please Note: For any *Pretty Woman* (1990) fans, this is the film (and the scene) that Vivian (Julia Roberts) is watching in the hotel suite before going downstairs to join Edward (Richard Gere) on the piano.

The Older Man: After many attempts by directors at pairing Audrey Hepburn and Cary Grant, Stanley Donen finally succeeded where William Wyler (*Roman Holiday*), Billy Wilder (*Sabrina Fair* and *Love In The Afternoon*) had failed and it was well worth the wait. Cary Grant had always been nervous of the twenty-five-year age gap between them. He agreed to be paired romantically with Audrey if the romance was twisted so that Audrey Hepburn was the aggressive pursuer and he the reluctant party. This made for a genuine strand of humour running through the film as witty gags were inserted into this thriller, making it a real pleasure to watch over and over again.

The Fashion: Despite a plot twist that leaves Audrey with only a few possessions in her holiday luggage, she is exquisitely dressed in Givenchy throughout the movie, from the opening shots of her in a sleek ski-suit and huge sunglasses, to a tailored black suit and white gloves.

The Verdict: In the style of one of the more lightweight Hitchcock films (*The 39 Steps*, *North By Northwest* for instance), *Charade* neatly blends comedy, romance and thrills to create one of the most perfect films. The plot twists and turns as does the mood, from suspense to slapstick, fear to surrealism, paranoia to chaos and violence to romance. It is one of the best (if not the best) of the romantic crime caper films so popular in the sixties.

The rapport between Cary Grant and Audrey Hepburn works perfectly - this is a sublime example of a director letting the chemistry between the two leads develop and then frame it with some ripe character acting from the rest of the cast. The film's final scene and use of the (then innovative and trendy) spilt screen as the couple carry on bickering even after 'The End' appears, makes a wonderful ending. 5/5

My Fair Lady (1964)

Cast: Audrey Hepburn (Eliza Doolittle), Rex Harrison (Professor Henry Higgins), Stanley Holloway (Alfred P Doolittle), Wilfred Hyde-White (Colonel Hugh Pickering), Gladys Cooper (Mrs Higgins), Jeremy Brett (Freddie Eynsford-Hill).

Crew: Director: George Cukor. Written by Alan Jay Lerner. Screenplay: Alan Jay Lerner. Original music: Frederick Lowe. Filmed in US. US. 170 minutes.

Story: Based on George Bernard Shaw's play *Pygmalion*, *My Fair Lady* is the ultimate 'Cinderella' story which continues to be remade over and over again - *Pretty Woman* (1990), *She's All That* (1999), *The Princess Diaries* (2001) and *Secretary* (2003) being among some of the most recent versions.

Eliza Doolittle (Audrey Hepburn) is busy selling flowers to a crowd of toffs leaving Covent Garden Opera House. Meanwhile, Professor Henry Higgins (Rex Harrison), a well-respected linguist, is making notes of street speech patterns. He meets Colonel Pickering (Wilfred Hyde-White) and boasts that he could turn 'this creature with her curb-stone English' into a 'Duchess at the Embassy Ball, or even get her a job as a lady's maid or shop assistant.' The next day Eliza turns up on their doorstep seeking elocution lessons and Pickering takes up Higgins' wager that within six months they could really pass Eliza off as a Duchess at an Embassy Ball. Eliza moves in and is put through a gruelling and punishing schedule of speech and deportment lessons.

Trial runs at Higgins' mothers and Ascot end in disaster, but they persist and finally everything falls into place just in time for the Embassy Ball. Higgins' experiment is put to the test when one of his former students is determined to discover who this mystery woman is and where she comes from. He announces that she is a fraud - that she is really a Hungarian princess. This pronouncement is whispered around the room until it reaches Higgins' ears whereupon he demands his money from Pickering. Their bet complete, he sees no use for Eliza anymore. Dejected, she walks out on him. Going back to Covent Garden, she finds she no longer belongs there. At Wimpole Street, Higgins and Pickering are confused by her departure but it soon becomes apparent that they miss her and that deep down Higgins might even love her. His encounter with Eliza has transformed him as well.

Background: Jack Warner paid an unprecedented $5.5 million for the film rights to Lerner's and Lowe's stage musical. Directed by George Cukor, it has more in common with a stage musical than a film. It was filmed in Super Panavision 70 at Burbank Studios, California. Cukor had originally hoped to film at Covent Garden, but this was ruled out as being too costly. After Warner's heavy initial investment, there were the cast and crew salaries to be considered. Audrey's fee was $1 million, the director George Cukor's was $300,000 and Rex

Harrison's was $200,000. The film finally came in at $17 million, but recovered that, plus a further $12 million on its initial release.

The film was nominated for twelve Oscars and won eight, but Audrey Hepburn was not even nominated for her magnificent performance. There had been much anti-Audrey press surrounding her engagement as Eliza Doolittle with many believing that the role should have gone to Julie Andrews who had wowed audiences in the West End and on Broadway. Audrey's $1 million salary had been widely reported as well. She was only the second woman ever to receive such a sum, matching Elizabeth Taylor's salary for *Cleopatra*.

Warners felt there was too much money to risk on an unknown stage performer and hired Audrey. Meanwhile, Disney snapped up Julie Andrews for *Mary Poppins* and it was Julie Andrews who won the Oscar for Best Actress. Strangely, everyone had forgotten that Audrey had been overlooked for the filmed version of her Broadway success *Gigi*!

We were lucky that Jack Warner, one of the last great movie moguls, didn't get his way in all the casting decisions. He initially approached James Cagney for the role of Alfred P Doolittle, but he wisely turned it down, knowing that he could never compete with Stanley Holloway who had made the role his own in the West End and on Broadway. Obviously aware of their success as sparring partners the previous year in *Charade*, Cary Grant was his first choice for Henry Higgins. Grant replied by saying that if they didn't ask Rex Harrison to recreate his stage role, he would never make a film for Warners again. Still convinced that Rex Harrison was too old (at fifty-five) and not a big enough name at the box office, they next offered the role to *Lawrence Of Arabia* star Peter O'Toole. He too turned it down so they finally offered the role to Rex Harrison who accepted and, although he had initial reservations about playing opposite Audrey Hepburn, he too was soon captivated by her charm.

Much of the backlash directed at Audrey was caused by the announcement that her singing had been dubbed. Audrey had thought that her voice was being used for all the songs. She had recorded them prior to filming and used them as 'playbacks' throughout the filming of the musical numbers. It was only when filming was near completion that she had discovered Marni Nixon had been secretly brought into the studio to re-record the numbers. She stormed off set for the first and only time during her career.

To coincide with the 1994 $600,000/six month restoration project on the film, a documentary entitled *Then And Now: The Making Of My Fair Lady* was made. In it, the documentary's narrator Jeremy Brett (re-creating *his* stage role) revealed that his songs had also been dubbed by Bill Shirley. Rex Harrison, on the other hand, refused to lip-synch: using a wireless mic in his tie, he sang live on set - each time creating a unique performance. This documentary also shows some clips of Audrey singing her own songs, alongside those of Marni Nixon, and Audrey's recordings are far superior as they are a continuation of acting performance rather than stand-alone songs.

Themes: **The Transformation:** The film's only flaw is that no matter how hard they tried to make Audrey look scruffy at the beginning: dirtying her clothes, matting her hair, plastering her face in mud and forcing dirt under her fingernails, she always looked exquisite. We are not surprised by the grand transformation, having seen it all before in *Sabrina Fair*, *Funny Face*, *Breakfast At Tiffany's* and others. Had an unknown such as Julie Andrews taken on the part, there would probably have been a keener sense of can she do it?

The film was shot in sequence to help Audrey in transforming herself from the dirty grimy flower-seller to supposed princess.

The Euphoric Moment: The transformation scene is at once her happiest moment and her most devastating. She worked hard to please Professor Higgins and Colonel Pickering and looks stunning in her antique ball-gown with her hair piled high. But they only congratulate themselves on their hard work and their achievement in turning this 'gutter snipe' into a 'lady'.

The Older Man: Another May to December romance, with Rex Harrison fifty-five to Audrey's thirty-five.

The Fashion: Cecil Beaton had designed the most beautiful costumes, hairstyles, jewellery and make-up for Audrey. However, the famous ball-gown was not a Beaton original but an antique dress he had found. He had known Audrey for some time. Indeed, it was at a party he had hosted in 1954 to celebrate the launch of *Roman Holiday* that she had met Mel Ferrer. He felt very proprietorial over her, believing he was grooming her for the role, rather than the film's director, George Cukor. The friction on set between them became so great, Cukor finally snapped and ordered Beaton off the set.

One of the film's great fashion sequences is the Ascot racing section where everyone is dressed in black and white or grey, except for Audrey who has a splash of colour on her dress. Humour is added when two women, wearing the same hat, bump into each other and back away in horror. Higgins, naturally, is the only one not dressed for Ascot, wearing a brown suit, which disgusts his mother.

Trivia: In 1914, when George Bernard Shaw's play *Pygmalion* was first staged - a huge furore broke out when Eliza Doolittle uttered the line, 'I washed my *bloody* face before I come, I did' - so much so that protesters petitioned Downing Street.

One of the constant criticisms levelled at Audrey Hepburn is her poor take on a cockney accent. Despite the film's image of one depicting Cockney life (i.e. East London), Eliza Doolittle actually comes from Lisson Grove in West London. She works in Covent Garden before taking up residence with Professor Higgins in Wimpole Street, both of which are in London's West End. We never once set foot in East London and many now heavily criticised 'cockney' accents in Hollywood movies are probably nearer the real pre-1939 thing than the 'mockney' accents used by many British actors today.

The women's loos on set had to be especially widened so that they could get in and out of them with their wide brim hats on.

Camellia Paglia said that this film is America's only frame of reference on the British class system. She believes that it was a huge success in the States, as they loved to see someone from the wrong side of the tracks unusually succeed and achieve in England - a common occurrence in American literature and real life.

The Verdict: This is a sumptuous and glorious big-screen musical of a most endearing stage musical. No expense was spared in recreating Covent Garden and a myriad of London buildings and streets. The extravagance of the costumes, settings, hairstyles and set dressings all add to Lerner's and Lowe's book to create a magnificent film. The performances are all exemplary, including the much-maligned Audrey. Considering her back catalogue of film set-ups where she transforms from ugly duckling to swan (most notably *Sabrina Fair* and *Funny Face*), this is a role that she was born to play. It is a shame that at the time there was so much adverse press surrounding her casting, her salary and Jack Warner's and George Cukor's foolish decision to dub Audrey's voice for the singing sequences. Audrey's songs may not have the oomph of Marni Nixon's, but they are far more pleasing, as they form part of Eliza's character development and should not have been seen as interchangeable stand-alone songs for the album release. It was a real shame the 30th anniversary film restoration didn't go as far as reinserting all Audrey's songs back into the soundtrack - perhaps on a 40th anniversary DVD release? 4/5

How To Steal A Million
(aka How To Steal A Million And Live Happily Ever After) (1966)

Cast: Audrey Hepburn (Nicole Bonnet), Peter O'Toole (Simon Dermott), Eli Wallach (Davis Leland), Hugh Griffith (Charles Bonnet), Charles Boyer (Charles De Solnay), Fernand Gravey (Grammont).

Crew: Director: William Wyler. Written by George Bradshaw and Harry Kurnitz. Filmed in Paris, France. US. 123 minutes.

Story: The original Nicole and Papa here, with Audrey Hepburn as Nicole Bonnet and Hugh Griffith as her father, Charles Bonnet: and yes, they do go round calling each other 'Nicole' and 'Papa'.

Charles Bonnet is an incredibly wealthy scoundrel and forger who at the start of the film sells one of his forged Cezanne paintings from his 'private' collection. His daughter, Nicole, is exasperated by his behaviour and warns that one day he'll get caught and then what would happen, as their entire family wealth is built on generations of top-notch art forgeries?

That one day looms ever closer when he decides to lend his Cellini Venus to the Lafayette Museum. Once installed, the museum's curator (Charles Boyer) realises it needs to be covered by special insurance and orders an expert in to appraise it. Meanwhile, Mr Leland (Eli Wallach), an American tycoon, takes an instant liking to the Venus and decides that at no matter what cost, he must possess it and orders an immediate investigation into the Bonnet family and its art collection...

Nicole has to devise a plan to save her and her father's reputation and fast. Salvation comes in the guise of Simon Dermott (Peter O'Toole), a man she believes to be an international art thief - well she did catch him red-handed in her house with one of her father's Van Goghs in his mitts. Between them they hatch a plan to pinch the Venus from the museum before the appraisal can be carried out.

The plan involves the two of them spending much of the film locked in a broom cupboard together. As you can imagine, a little more than art theft transpires... But is Dermott really a thief? What is Leland up to? And how do you steal a million and live happily ever after?

Background: In 1964, after an extended period travelling with Mel as an attempt to hold their marriage together, she was keen to settle down once again, especially now Sean was reaching school age. Eventually, she discovered the village of Tolochenaz overlooking Lake Geneva and bought a house there. This would remain her primary residence until her death.

In July 1965, eager to make another film, she agreed to work with William Wyler once again on this romantic heist movie, which was to be shot in her favourite city, Paris.

Filming was fun and Peter O'Toole and Audrey look as though they had enjoyed working together, although the film was not the hit they had all hoped it would be. It was especially hard for Audrey whose first film this was since her unhappy experiences on *My Fair Lady*.

Themes: **The Euphoric Moment:** The scenes where Nicole and Simon are locked in the museum broom cupboard waiting for the precise moment to carry out their raid are some of the funniest and sexiest scenes in any movie. Wyler, as reported in Barry Paris' biography of Hepburn, said that, 'They [Hepburn and O'Toole] react on each other like laughing gas, and the trouble is they're in almost every scene together.' Their obvious delight at playing so close to each other, on the verge of near constant laughter, makes for some truly delightful screen moments.

The Older Woman: Despite still playing the young chit of a girl, Audrey is three years older than her leading man, Peter O'Toole.

The Fashion: As part of the plan, Dermott asks Nicole to change into drab clothes - indignantly she asks, 'What for?' His reply? 'For one thing it gives Givenchy the night off.'

Givenchy once again created her wardrobe, including some really odd outfits, which have more in common with the then currently fashionable 'kookie' creations from London's Kings Road, rather than Parisian high fashion. Her first appearance is a true expression of the film's sense of fun and an embracing of the swinging sixties (The Beatles were at the top of the hit parade in 1964). Audrey is seen driving a red sports car, whilst wearing all white: suit, gloves, hat and sunglasses.

Trivia: Art director, Alexander Trauner, had to create a museum full of fake paintings and sculptures for the movie. As part of the film's marketing strategy, these were later shown at Paris and New York and featured in *Life* magazine.

George C Scott was originally cast as David Leland but was fired for being late.

The Verdict: Much like the film's central premise, this is no real work of art. It is a light frothy piece of fun. Capturing the spirit of the time, it is an ephemeral film, but there is nothing wrong with that. It's great to see Peter O'Toole at his most handsome and suave playing the fool to Audrey at her most modern and charming. The obvious pleasure the two leads had in filming is evident on the screen and, as they spend so much time together, this is a real bonus. The supporting cast, particularly Hugh Griffith, Charles Boyer and Eli Wallach, add to the film's overall frivolity. A tad long at a little over two hours, but that's a small price to pay for such a treasure. 4½/5

Two For The Road (1967)

Cast: Audrey Hepburn (Joanna Wallace), Albert Finney (Mark Wallace), Eleanor Bron (Cathy Manchester), William Daniels (Howard Manchester), Gabrielle Middleton (Ruth Manchester), Claude Dauphin (Maurice Dalbret).

Crew: Director: Stanley Donen. Written by Frederic Raphael. Filmed in rural France and the Riviera. US. 111 minutes.

Story: A fractious couple, Mark and Joanna Wallace (Albert Finney and Audrey Hepburn) return from a short motoring holiday in the South of France and reminisce on their annual holidays in France over their twelve years together. With a voice-over commentary to guide the viewer through this complex and fragmented story, we see them as young students in the year they met. Over subsequent years we see the decline of their marriage with episodes such as the year the MG fell apart; the year they travelled with another married couple and their brat; the year of executive stress; the year he travelled alone and met a vivacious blonde; the year with their young daughter, the year she had an affair;

the year he tried to make her jealous. Over the years we see that wealth and success have not brought them happiness: the final two words in the film are 'bitch' and 'bastard'.

Background: Audrey turned down a $1 million offer to appear with Peter O'Toole again - in the musical remake of *Goodbye Mr Chips* (the part went to Petula Clark) - to work with her *Funny Face* and *Charade* director, Stanley Donen in Frederic Raphael's chronicle of a marriage in decay. This must have been especially hard for Audrey whose marriage was on its final legs following her recent third miscarriage.

The film's narrative structure was radical and the film moves between the twelve years of the Wallace marriage - as they in effect pass themselves on the same road, year in year out. This was a film that owed more to the conceits of the French New Wave than the Hollywood comedies and dramas Audrey had been used to. As she was entering a new phase in her private life, she embraced this new style and plunged into the project. Her salary for the film was $750,000; Finney's was $300,000.

Filming took place entirely in rural France and on the Riviera between May and October 1966, and was released nine months later to mixed reviews.

Themes: **The Transformation:** The whole film is a transformation as we see Audrey across a decade from a make-up-less woman to a pigtailed eighteen-year-old. Only an actress such as Audrey could get away with this conceit. This was her first film where she was allowed to play a woman nearer her age. Even in her previous film, *How To Steal A Million*, she was still effectively playing the girl. Here, she was allowed to both grow up and grow young at the same time. It was the perfect transition movie for Audrey. But the adult Audrey, without make-up and Givenchy outfits, who occasionally swears, was a little too much for the public and critics to accept. It is a brave performance that deserves far better praise than it usually gets.

The Euphoric Moment: *Two For The Road* is the journey of a marriage, and as such, there are ups and downs, and as the marriage progresses and worsens, there are more downs than ups. But one of the key euphoric vignettes is when their car breaks down and they push it to a large hotel. The room price is astronomical. In order to save money, Mark ventures out to get hold of some food to avoid eating in the hotel's expensive restaurant. When he returns, they are like naughty children having a midnight feast.

The Older Woman: Audrey is seven years older than her leading man, Albert Finney, but that didn't stop the magic both on- and off-screen as there were rumours of an affair - which was one of the contributing factors to her marriage break-up.

The Fashion: Stanley Donen was insistent that Givenchy must not be involved in this project. The film is spread over twelve years and demands that Audrey age backwards from her thirties to her teens. This would be shown through her performance, hair, make-up and the clothes she would have been able to afford at various stages in her life. With Lady Rendlesham acting as adviser, Audrey is seen wearing various 'off-the-peg' clothes of designers including Ken Scott, Michele Rosier, Paco Rabanne, Mary Quant, Foale and Tuffin.

Trivia: Paul Newman had originally been offered the role of Mark Wallace.

The Verdict: A much-underrated film, with a major harsher and harder role for Audrey. She had dared to grow up and audiences and critics were not (and are still not) ready to accept this. Coupled with the film's complex narrative structure and independent European flavour, rather than Hollywood gloss, it is a real contrast to most of the other films in Audrey's oeuvre. A shining example of the swinging sixties, with the then popular Frederic Raphael's script and concept - but perhaps a bit too modish at times. It hasn't dated well but it does contain real moments of pain side by side with genuine humour. A fascinating look at married life. 4/5

Wait Until Dark (1967)

Cast: Audrey Hepburn (Suzy Hendrix), Alan Arkin (Roat/Harry Roat Jr/Roat Sr), Richard Crenna (Mike Talman), Efrem Zimbalist Jr (Sam Hendrix), Jack Weston (Carlino), Samantha Jones (Liza).

Crew: Director: Terence Young. Written by Frederick Knott and Robert Howard-Carrington. Producer: Mel Ferrer. Filmed in US and Canada. US. 107 minutes.

Story: A similar set-up to *Charade* (just without the laughs or the romance): everyone is after the money that they think Suzy (Audrey Hepburn) has, but instead, she has unwittingly passed it on to an innocent child...

Liza (Samantha Jones) is smuggling heroin into the US stuffed inside a porcelain doll. Suspecting that she has been double-crossed by her boss, Harry Roat (Alan Arkin), she drops the doll into Sam Hendrix's (Efrem Zimbalist Jr) bag. Returning home to his recently blinded wife, Suzy, he gives her the doll, before going off on another trip.

Whilst away, the nasty Roat concocts a series of evil schemes in order to get his hands back on the heroin-filled doll.

Background: Negotiations had begun in June 1965 for Audrey to star in a screen adaptation of Frederick Knott's thriller *Wait Until Dark*, which had been a huge hit on Broadway with Lee Remick in the central role. Filming finally began in January 1967 and would be split between Warner Brothers' studios in California, and location work in New York and Toronto. Audrey was to earn her now standard fee of $750,000 plus 10% of the gross, her expenses would be $1,000 per week and Mel would pick up $50,000 as the film's producer. It was directed by Terence Young of James Bond fame and he would earn $250,000 plus $25,000 expenses.

In part, this must have been another last-ditch attempt to save the Hepburn/Ferrer marriage as Mel was working behind the scenes as producer. It was shot on location in New York and Toronto and the interiors were filmed at the Warner Studios in Hollywood.

As Sean was now at school, he had to stay behind in Switzerland, which made Audrey nervous and she was constantly phoning home. Mel was on the move again which compounded rumours of their marriage collapse, especially as his name had been linked to several European lovelies. Audrey, a lady to the end, refused to be drawn into gossip, even in such a gossip-fuelled town as Hollywood.

The film opened in October 1967 and was an instant box office success, taking $11 million. Audrey, who had worked so hard researching her role as a blind woman, received an extra bonus when she was nominated for her fifth Best Actress Oscar. But this success was tinged with sadness for in the winter of 1967/68, she and Mel finally split up. They were divorced in November 1968.

Themes: **The Transformation:** No physical transformation. Suzy is bullied and taunted by the evil Roat in an attempt to find out how much she knows about the missing heroin. In the early scenes she is a newly blinded, insecure but independent woman - by the end she has become strong, and defeats the bad guys on her own. It is only when she has laid them out that her husband comes to the rescue.

The Older Man: No real love interest in the film as her husband, played by Efrem Zimbalist Jr, is absent for much of the movie, only coming to the rescue once she has triumphed.

Behind the scenes is a different matter, with Mel Ferrer as producer trying to keep their marriage going despite Audrey's affair with Finney the previous year.

Trivia: George C Scott and Robert Redford had both been offered the part of Roat before Alan Arkin accepted.

The Verdict: Acting blind must be one of the toughest acting challenges there can be and Audrey pulls if off with great skill and style, earning herself her fifth Academy Award Nomination in the process. However, even by 1968 standards it is incredibly dated. 1968 was the turning point in Hollywood as the self-regulatory Production Code set up in the 1930s had been abolished, the Hollywood Studio System had collapsed and as a result, a new breed of film-makers, actors and performances were infiltrating. This was the year of *The Graduate, Rosemary's Baby* and *The Detective* - gritty, raw films which had a real edge to them. *Wait Until Dark,* although dark and nasty, seems too stagy and old-school by these standards. 3/5

Housewife And Mother (1968-1976)

Throughout 1968, Audrey spent the year resting and spending time with her son, as preparations were underway for her divorce.

Over the summer, she had been holidaying on a Greek island with millionaire Paul Weiller and his wife, Princess Olympia Torlonia, and it was there that she met Dr Andrea Dotti, a handsome, aristocratic and charming Italian psychiatrist. His family had considerable reservations about the marriage: Audrey was not Roman Catholic; she was about to be a divorcee; she was ten years older than their son and, of particular concern, her health might prevent them from gaining a grandson. Her concerns focused solely on Sean's reaction to Andrea as a step-father.

Finally, all problems were overcome and they married in January 1969.

Audrey was determined that she would put Andrea and Sean before her career and 'retired' from acting to pursue a career as mother and wife in Andrea's home city - Rome.

By the spring of 1969, she was pregnant and, keen that there could be no chance of miscarrying, Audrey moved back to Switzerland and spent her pregnancy resting at her home there. Her strategy paid off and her second son (Luca) was born in February 1970.

However, the marriage was stretched to near breaking point during this long separation. Andrea was only able to visit at weekends, and then not every one. Rumours that he had been photographed escorting a model to public events in Rome had reached Audrey and so she returned to Rome.

It was now the 1970s and times had changed. The Hollywood Studio System had collapsed and a new young breed of film-makers had emerged bringing with them new actors and performance styles from the stage and TV. Movie stars of the Golden Age were no longer in vogue and no suitable offers materialised. All that changed when she was offered *Robin And Marian*.

Robin And Marian (1976)

Cast: Sean Connery (Robin Hood), Audrey Hepburn (Lady Marian), Robert Shaw (Sheriff of Nottingham), Richard Harris (King Richard), Nicol Williamson (Little John), Denholm Elliott (Will Scarlett), Ronnie Barker (Friar Tuck), Ian Holm (King John).

Crew: Director: Richard Lester. Written by James Goldman. Filmed in Spain. US. 106 minutes.

Story: Robin Hood: Twenty-Five Years Later.

When King Richard (Richard Harris) dies, Robin Hood (Sean Connery) and Little John (Nicol Williamson) have lost their favourite adversary and decide that after twenty-odd years of theft and battle, it is time to retire.

Where else would they retire than back to the Midlands and Sherwood Forest? There, they meet with two faces from their past: Will Scarlett (Denholm Elliott) and Friar Tuck (Ronnie Barker) who fill them in on all the gossip...

The Sheriff of Nottingham (Robert Shaw) is up to his old tricks and the new king, King John (Ian Holm) has divided the country and spends all day in bed with his twelve-year-old wife. Although all this is of interest, Robin only wants to know what has happened to Maid Marian (Audrey Hepburn).

It transpires that Marian is now an Abbess at Kirklee Abbey. When Robin arrives there, she is patiently waiting to be arrested by the evil Sheriff of Nottingham as part of King John's policy of rounding up the senior clergy. At this point, Robin comes out of retirement and insists on rescuing her, much to her chagrin.

In revenge, the Sheriff of Nottingham kidnaps all the other nuns, forcing Robin to come to his castle for one final showdown.

Background: Audrey was drawn to the 'beautifully written script' by James Goldman, in whose *Lion In Winter* Katharine Hepburn had had such success in 1968. It also gave her the chance to play a woman of her own age. An extra incentive was to star opposite Sean Connery, or James Bond, as he was known to her two sons.

During her absence from films, she found that much had changed. What she hoped would be a fun and gentle return to film turned into an experience where she had to overcome and confront many obstacles. The film Audrey had signed up for was a mature romance, but increasingly the male-dominated cast and crew were focusing far more on the action, and the romance began to disappear. Richard Lester was one of the new breed of film-makers who had come to the film industry from TV commercials. Audrey found Lester's try-it-and-see approach to film-making hard to adjust to, and now aged fifty-seven and with a nine-year gap from the cameras, she was finding this constant high-pressure pace hard going.

For Lester, it was also one of his toughest assignments. For him, it was nothing to do with the script (although he did say in interview: 'Filming *Superman* wasn't hard, filming forty-five pages of script with two people sitting under an oak tree talking - now that's tough.') the locations or the cast, but the bane in most directors' life, the 'money men'.

The film's below-the-line budget of under a million had escalated to $6 million by the end. Lester blamed this on the excesses of the film's producers, Stark and Sheppard, who were paid $2.5 million for their services to the film - 'They came down once, said hello once to me, had lunch with Audrey and went to Biarritz for ten days and charged the whole bloody thing to our overheads.'

Lester had completed what he felt was the rough edit of the film, but Columbia had other plans, deciding that the film should be aimed at a family audience and demanded a series of cuts to make this possible. Lester, who didn't have a final cut contract had to see some of the more hard-hitting sequences removed, including a shot of an arrow going in an eye and a corpse in uniform being hacked to bits. It was also given a score (by John Barry) that he believed sounded epic - whereas to him the whole aim of the film was to be an anti-epic along the lines of Robert Altman's 1971 western *McCabe And Mrs Miller*.

The film premiered at Radio City Music Hall and Audrey was cheered by thousands of waiting fans on her arrival. However, the critics were not so kind and the film was critically mauled.

Nor was her marriage in great shape. Regular press coverage of Andrea's playboy lifestyle was compounded by a kidnap attempt on Andrea. He escaped unharmed but Audrey, fearing for her children, fled to Switzerland where she suffered another miscarriage.

Themes: **The Fashion:** Back in the habit again! All costumes were designed by Yvonne Blake.

Trivia: Denholm Elliott didn't stay at the hotel with the rest of the cast and crew; he preferred the solace of a monastery - which served wine.

One of the film's most important scenes had to be reshot as the speed of the stock used had been incorrect. In *Getting Away With It or: The Further Adventures Of The Luckiest Bastard You Ever Saw*, Steven Soderbergh and Richard Lester reminisce: '[It was] the night scene with Nicol Williamson and Audrey Hepburn, and the camp's in the background ... And Nicol was wonderful. I loved it, the way he did it. But you couldn't see Audrey's hair at all ... Just her face floating [like] a kind of Cheshire Cat that was moving around in the dark, it looked absolutely dreadful, so we reshot it and he got the balance right and it was just warmed over stew, you know. Sometimes a casserole is better the next day, but a lot of food isn't. We just went back to the original and said to the lab, "Do what you can".'

The Verdict: This is not a big action film. There are some startling set pieces, including the showdown between Robin and the Sheriff of Nottingham. Despite the money-makers' attempts to change the film's slant, it is still a cerebral and somewhat elegiac story of two lovers reunited after twenty-five years. That they happen to be Robin Hood and Maid Marian is secondary. 3/5

Sidney Sheldon's Bloodline (1979)

Cast: Audrey Hepburn (Elizabeth Roffe), Ben Gazzara (Rhys Williams), James Mason (Sir Alec Nichols), Omar Sharif (Ivo Palazzi), Claudia Mori (Donatella), Irene Papas (Simonetta Palazzi), Michelle Phillips (Vivian Nichols).

Crew: Director: Terence Young. Written by Laird Doenig. Filmed in New York, Copenhagen, Rome, Munich, London, Paris, Zurich and Sardinia. US/ West Germany. 116 minutes.

Story: When Sam Roffe dies in a freak mountaineering accident, his vulture-like family descend to fight over the family fortune. His daughter Elizabeth (Audrey Hepburn) gains control of the business but her cousins, who are also shareholders, are eager to get their hands on the money by turning the company into a PLC.

When it transpires the rope on which Sam was relying whilst climbing had been severed by a bullet, the 'accident' becomes a murder investigation with the entire family on trial. Elizabeth and her father's business friend, Rhys Williams (Ben Gazzara), go to Zurich to investigate, and their relationship becomes more friendship than business.

Meanwhile, scattered across Europe, we begin to see the seedy world beneath the rich Euro-facade as the cousins' dirty secrets become clear. Sex 'n' snuff movies, young trophy wives with large gambling debts, and failed businesses could all be possible motives to murder... But when the brakes on Elizabeth's car are sabotaged and a young woman dies in a lift-shaft drama, the questions are who can Elizabeth trust and is the murderer closer to her than it at first appears?

Background: Terence Young, with whom she had worked so effectively on *Wait Until Dark,* lured Audrey back to the big screen for *Sidney Sheldon's Bloodline,* a big-budget international pot-boiler. With a budget of $12 million created by a strange quirk in the Bonn's tax-break laws (even if the film lost money, the money men would be quids in), filming took place across Europe. Audrey was paid $1 million plus a percentage of the profits. She also arranged to do most of the scenes in Rome so as to be away from home as little as possible. Not that she stayed at home; she stayed at the Grand Hotel - another sign to the waiting press that her second marriage was on the rocks.

The film opened to dreadful reviews. For example, *The Sunday Express* said that it was 'ghastly, hackneyed, humourless, grubby and ... so disjointed as to be a pain to follow'.

Themes: **The Transformation:** Much like her role in her previous collaboration with Young in *Wait Until Dark*, the transformation is from dependent woman to strong independent woman. The transformation is internal rather than an external reflection. Elizabeth, at the beginning of the film, is a sheltered and pampered palaeontologist. By the end she is standing in her father's footsteps demanding and getting the respect.

The Older Woman: In Sidney Sheldon's novel, the character Audrey plays was twenty-three years old. Sidney Sheldon, so keen to secure Audrey for the lead after his first choices of Jacqueline Bisset, Candice Bergen and Diane Keaton had all declined the role, agreed to change the character's age to thirty-five in the paperback edition.

This is the first of two films where Audrey is paired opposite Ben Gazzara (she is one year older than he is). Rumours abounded of an off-screen romance. This worried Andrea so much that a 'second honeymoon' was ordered. But it was too little too late and by the time Audrey and Ben worked together on *They All Laughed*, the marriage had ended and they divorced in 1983.

The Fashion: There were fourteen lavish 'power-dressing' outfits designed for the film by Givenchy, including a selection of simple tailored suits, an evening black dinner suit and a beaded evening dress. The rest of the film's costumes were designed by Enrico Sabbatini.

The Verdict: With James Mason, Audrey Hepburn and Omar Sharif in one movie, you'd be up for thinking that you are in for a cracking yarn to while away a couple of hours. But this is a huge Euro-pudding of a movie: large international cast, exotic locations, bluffs and double bluffs a plenty - but to be quite frank, who really cares when it is all so dull and nasty. Pornography, snuff movies, serial murders and women having their knees nailed to the ground by loan sharks are just some of the highlights to be 'enjoyed' in this unsavoury tosh. 0/5

They All Laughed (1981)

Cast: Audrey Hepburn (Angela Niotes), Ben Gazzara (John Russo), Patti Hansen (Sam/Deborah Wilson), John Ritter (Charles Rutledge), Dorothy Stratten (Dolores Martin), Blaine Novak (Arthur Brodsky), Sean Ferrer (Jose), Colleen Camp (Christy).

Crew: Director: Peter Bogdanovich. Written by Peter Bogdanovich. Filmed in New York. US. 115 minutes.

Story: The film is set over one weekend in New York, and follows the antics of three private eyes and their various romantic entanglements.

John Russo (Ben Gazzara), Charles Rutledge (John Ritter) and Arthur Brodsky (Blaine Novak) are three private investigators following two separate women: Angela Niotes (Audrey Hepburn) and a mysterious blonde, Dolores Martin (Dorothy Stratten).

Charles falls for Dolores, the beautiful blonde. John falls first for a country singer, Christy (Colleen Camp), then a glamorous cab driver he insists on calling Sam (Patti Hansen) before finally coming to his senses and falling for Angela, the wife of his client - who he has been hired to follow. Meanwhile, Dolores' cuckolded boyfriend, Jose, falls for Christy!

The various entanglements eventually sort themselves out and John, who started out as an uncaring ladies' man, ends up with a broken heart but a comfortable shoulder to cry on.

Background: Audrey's keenness to work with Ben Gazzara once again must have been a key reason in taking on the role of a bored wife to a tycoon. Bogdanovich had been the golden boy of Hollywood during the 1970s but was now better known for his private life. Indeed, the film is dedicated to Dorothy Stratten, the former Playboy model who was murdered by her estranged husband (who then killed himself) while the film was in post-production. She was having an affair with Peter Bogdanovich at the time of her death. He later wrote her biography *The Killing Of The Unicorn* published in 1984 and then married her sister!

As a consequence, this frothy comedy received a poor reception. It also pretty much put an end to Bogdanovich's career as he had to declare bankruptcy following his personal investment of $5 million in releasing and distributing the film. It went on to gross less than $1 million.

Filming took place in New York, and it was while there that Audrey met Robert Wolders, who was to become her companion until her death.

Themes: **The Older Woman:** Audrey's second film with Ben Gazzara, one year her junior. By the time the film was coming to its close, so was their affair.

The Fashion: No Givenchy: blue jeans, silk shirt and jacket - real clothes for a real mother, but my, doesn't she make them look stylish.

Trivia: The title for *They All Laughed* was borrowed from a Gershwin song composed for Fred Astaire and Ginger Rogers in *Shall We Dance* (1937).

The Verdict: I assume this is meant to be some kind of farce, in the manner of Woody Allen, given the clue in the film's title '*They All Laughed*' - I'm not quite sure who 'They' are but I certainly didn't. It was written with Audrey Hepburn in mind as a light, but at the same time melancholic, look at love and relationships. However, it fails on all levels. It is neither funny, romantic nor thought-provoking. The highly experienced Gazzara and Audrey received only a bit of support from John Ritter (fresh from his TV success in *The Waltons*), otherwise they had to carry an ex-pretend playboy model (Colleen Camp in *Apocalypse Now!*), a real playboy model (the sadly tragic Dorothy Stratten) and two complete unknowns (Patti Hansen and Blaine Novak) with, it would appear, only half-hearted direction. The film therefore, has a sadly unpolished look. Audrey does get to work with her eldest son though. Considering the disastrous post-production and release, it is not really a surprise, but a shame as this was Audrey's last lead role in a feature film. 1/5

4. Special Guest Star ... Audrey Hepburn

Always (1989)

Cast: Audrey Hepburn (Hap), Richard Dreyfuss (Pete Sandrich), Holly Hunter (Dorinda Durston), Brad Johnson (Ted Baker), John Goodman (Al Yackey), Robert Blossom (Dave), Keith David (Powerhouse), Marg Helgenberger (Rachel), Dale Dye (Fire Boss), Doug McGrath (Bus Driver).

Crew: Director: Steven Spielberg. Producers: Kathleen Kennedy, Frank Marshall and Steven Spielberg. Screenplay: Jerry Belson. Based on the screenplay for *A Guy Named Joe* by Dalton Trumbo. Filmed in US. US. 106 minutes.

Story: Audrey Hepburn's final film appearance was in Steven Spielberg's remake of the 1943 film *A Guy Named Joe*. She has a small but pivotal role of an angel, Hap, guiding Pete (Richard Dreyfuss) through the first few months after his death. He is a lost soul on Earth, unable to let go of his one true love, Dorinda (Holly Hunter), and as such, preventing her from forming a new relationship with the hunky Ted Baker (Brad Johnson).

Pete died in a plane crash on the very day he promised to quit his cavalier and downright dangerous attitude to flying, fire-fighting and training pilots how to put out fires. But first he has to go on 'one last call' and it literally would be his last as he dies saving his best friend, Al Yackey's (John Goodman), life.

In a lush green forest, he comes across an elegant woman dressed from top to toe in white. As she cuts his hair he says, 'Either I'm dead or crazy.' The angel's response, 'Well, you're not crazy.' She tells him that he will be trapped in the in-between world until he lets go of the past. He is tasked with providing inspiration to a new pilot, Ted, and to ensure that Dorinda's life doesn't end just as his has.

Background: The original 1943 screenplay was written by Dalton Trumbo who had written *Roman Holiday*. Spielberg and team were keen to recreate some nostalgic relationship between the two and felt that Audrey would be ideal as the angel as it was a role she had been carrying out in real-life for UNICEF. She spent some time working (by phone) with Spielberg's writing team, moulding the role especially for her. She spent ten days working with Spielberg for a reported $1 million fee, most of which she turned over to UNICEF. Despite being little more than a cameo, Universal lobbied for a Best Supporting Actress nomination at the Academy Awards for her, but it was not to be.

Trivia: The part of Hap was originally intended for her *Robin And Marian* co-star Sean Connery.

The Verdict: Despite being overly sentimental at times, this is one of Spielberg's more mature efforts at getting to the heart of love and life. The performances of the four key actors: Holly Hunter, Richard Dreyfuss, John Goodman and Brad Johnson, are all good at treading that fine line between melodrama and realism. The stunt sequences of the planes and fires are all exceptional given that it was made in the days before Computer Generated Imagery. For Audrey, it was a perfect swansong. 4/5

5. And Tonight On Television ...
Audrey Hepburn

Mayerling (1957)

Cast: Audrey Hepburn (Marie Vetseva), Mel Ferrer (Crown Prince Rudolf von Habsburg), Raymond Massey (Prince Rudolf's Father), Diana Wynyard (Prince Rudolf's Mother).

Crew: Director: Anatole Litvak. Screenplay: Claude Anet. NBC TV. Filmed in New York. US. 90 minutes.

Story: Based on the true story of the Crown Prince Rudolf of Austria who fell in love with a seventeen-year-old courtesan, Marie. Rather than part, they made a suicide pact.

Background: Shot in New York over eighteen days in January 1957 (it was transmitted two weeks later), *Mayerling* was the biggest budget extravaganza television had ever seen. It had a budget of $620,000, a cast of over a hundred, and lavish sets and costumes. Audrey received the highest fee paid to any performer for a television drama, at that point, $157,000.

Directed by Anatole Litvak, it is an almost word-for-word remake of his 1936 version starring Charles Boyer and Danielle Darrieux as the doomed couple. The film received a limited European cinema release the following year.

Trivia: Audrey Hepburn was reportedly distraught when Catherine Deneuve was cast opposite Omar Sharif in the big screen adaptation of *Mayerling* in 1968. But as Audrey would have been nearly forty, even she would have had a big job in passing herself as seventeen.

The Verdict: Although critics had high expectations of this television drama, they failed to materialise. The criticism fell largely on Mel's shoulders and the lack of passion between the couple, who although married in real-life, did not convey the grand passion needed for the roles. As critic John Crosby put it, 'The lovers seem fated to bore each other to death rather than to end their illicit alliance in a murder-suicide pact.'

Love Among Thieves (1987)

Cast: Audrey Hepburn (Baroness Caroline Dulac), Robert Wagner (Mr Chambers), Samantha Eggar (Solange DuLac), Patrick Bauchan (Alan Channing).

Crew: Director: Roger Young. Written by Stephen Black and Henry Stern. Filmed in Paris, San Francisco and Tuscon. US. 91 minutes.

Story: Baroness Caroline Dulac (Audrey Hepburn), world-renowned concert pianist, is giving a concert at a museum when a priceless collection of Faberge eggs is stolen. But lo, the thief is wearing gold strappy sandals identical to those of our heroine. With the eggs safely hidden in her evening bag, we soon discover that her fiancé, Alan Channing (Patrick Bauchan), is being held hostage and she has been forced to steal the eggs in order to secure his release.

A mishap with a vicious thug leaves her shaken but with instructions to fly to Madeira to exchange the eggs for her fiancé. This brings her into contact with Mr Chambers (Robert Wagner) - an unpleasant cigar-smoking, beer-swilling pain. Naturally, they take an instant dislike to each another. So the stage is set for the perfect screwball comedy/road movie as the two of them are forced to share the only hire car on a 200-mile drive from Madeira airport to the 'drop' in Ledera. Along the way they get accosted by bandits and Chambers trades the lovely Baroness for 200 hand-rolled Cuban cigars. Their subsequent late-night escape ends in disaster and she misses the midnight exchange deadline. She is on the run once again - with Chambers in hot pursuit. Eventually she meets up with the thugs holding her fiancé hostage and is forced to confront a situation far worse than anything she has had to encounter in her secure titled world.

Background: Audrey was lured back to the screen (small, not big this time) for a TV movie for Lorimer starring opposite Robert Wagner for the 'fun of it' and her usual $750,000 fee. Givenchy created two outfits for her to wear in the film: a black and white gown at the beginning of the film and a red one at the end.

Filming took place in Tuscon, Arizona, where temperatures reached 102 degrees. Unfortunately, the film's reception was not so hot, with most reviewers being unnecessarily harsh. The *New Yorker* said, '*Love Among Thieves* wants to be witty and just sits there with drool.'

The Verdict: Certainly not as bad as *They All Laughed* or *Sidney Sheldon's Bloodline*. This is your standard murder/mystery/road/romance movie with two engaging leads having fun and carrying out their roles with gumption. There is a genuine rapport between the two of them. Indeed, Audrey confessed that she was a huge *Hart To Hart* fan and the warmth generated makes for an amiable hour or so. 3/5

Gardens Of The World With Audrey Hepburn
(1993)

Cast: Audrey Hepburn (Host), Michael York (Narrator).

Crew: Producer: Janis Blackshleger. Director: Bruce Franchini. US. 30 minutes (8 episodes).

Who better to stroll around the Gardens of the World with but Audrey Hepburn. And so in April 1990, Audrey found herself back in Holland for tulip season. Other places visited in the series included Mottisfont Abbey in Hampshire, the Dominican Republic, Tuscany, Saiho-ji in Kyoto and the Jardins de Luxembourg in Paris. In each garden, she examines the garden's style and philosophy. The six-part series was split into botanical genres: 'Roses and Rose Gardens', 'Tulips and Spring Bulbs', 'Formal Gardens', 'Flowers and Flower Gardens', 'Country Gardens' and 'Public Gardens'.

There was an accompanying book, for which Audrey Hepburn wrote the foreword, published in 1991 by Macmillan, entitled *Gardens Of The World: The Art And Practice Of Gardening* edited by Penelope Hobhouse and Elvin McDonald.

6. Theatrical Productions

High Buttoned Shoes (1948)

Cast: Included Lew Parker, Kay Kimber and Sid James.

Crew: Score: Jule Styne. Choreographer: Jerome Robbins.

Story: Set in the 1920s, the loose plot concerns the escapades of a con man. The dance numbers were based on those of the period with the Charleston heavily featured, and the on-screen antics of the Keystone Cops and Sennett's Bathing Beauties.

Background: Four hundred girls had auditioned for the chorus and Audrey was one of the forty cast. *High Buttoned Shoes* opened at the London Hippodrome on 22 December 1948. It ran for 291 performances, closing in May 1949. Despite being offered £20 a week, Audrey declined to go on the national tour.

It was at this point that she stopped her ballet classes at the Ballet Rambert school, and instead began private acting lessons with Felix Aylmer.

Trivia: Most of the Audrey Hepburn biographies (and indeed the recent film *The Audrey Hepburn Story*) claim that Audrey and the British comedienne Kay Kendall appeared together in *High Buttoned Shoes*. This is disputed by Kay Kendall's biographer (Eve Golden). In her book, *The Brief, Madcap Life Of Kay Kendall*, written with Kay's sister Kim, it says that they never performed together but were bosom buddies in their private lives when they went clubbing together.

Sauce Tartare (1949), Sauce Piquante (1950)

Cast: Included Bob Monkhouse, Norman Wisdom, Marcel le Bon and Douglas Byng.

Crew: Producer: Cecil Landau.

Background: After her chorus line work in *High Buttoned Shoes* had come to an end, she went immediately into two consecutive revues produced by Cecil Landau at the Cambridge Theatre.

Gradually she was promoted from pretty young thing in the chorus to walk-on parts in the comedians' sketches.

It was during this period that gossip columnists and theatre reviewers started 'discovering' her, and she also did a spot of modelling during the day. One such shoot was for Lux soap. The image is still popular today and is reproduced on countless postcards (just with the soap airbrushed out).

Whilst working on these two revues she began her first serious relationship - with the French singer Marcel le Bon, but it fizzled out by the end of the run.

Landau took a truncated version of the revue to Ciro's night-club where it began a short run as a late-night cabaret show. Audrey was one of the lucky dancers to transfer there with the show. Now audiences could see her close up rather than from the back of the stalls.

It was whilst performing there that she was spotted by Mario Zampi, the producer of *Laughter In Paradise*. He cast her in a small role, and so her movie career was born.

Gigi (1951)

Cast: Audrey Hepburn (Gigi), Cathleen Nesbitt (Aunt Alicia), Josephine Brown (Madame Alvarez).

Crew: Producer: Gilbert Miller. Based on the novel by Colette. Adapted by Anita Loos.

Story: In this two-act play set in Paris in 1900, based on Colette's novel and adapted by Anita Loos, Gigi is a shy and gawky teenage girl. Her mother is a mediocre soprano at the Opera Comique and coquette, and it is expected that Gigi will follow into the family business. But she is more interested in studying and has little time or interest in learning the tricks of the trade.

Background: There are conflicting show business stories surrounding how Colette met and fell for her 'Gigi'. However, this meeting did take place whilst Audrey was in Monte Carlo filming *Monte Carlo Baby* and Colette did work hard at convincing Gilbert Miller that this unknown actress was Broadway material. But as Colette had retained casting approval over the actress to play the title role, Audrey was finally cast.

Having had no legitimate theatrical training, Audrey found it difficult at first to carry off this demanding role. But her co-star, Cathleen Nesbitt, gave Hepburn private coaching in order to extend the range of her voice to ensure that even those in the balcony could hear.

When the play opened in Philadelphia in November 1951, reviews were mixed. But three weeks later when they opened at Broadway's Fulton Theatre, the reviews were ecstatic, most aimed at newcomer Audrey Hepburn. Overnight, the theatre's neon sign was adjusted to reflect the reviews, Audrey received her first above-the-title credit, and later, a Tony (Broadway's Oscars) for Best Actress.

Despite huge box office demand, *Gigi* finished its Broadway run in May 1952 in order for Audrey to fulfil her contract with Paramount to star in *Roman Holiday*, which had already been delayed due to the play's success. She returned to the role for a long coast-to-coast tour of the play in 1953.

The Verdict: '[Audrey Hepburn gave] a wonderfully bouncy performance which establishes her as an actress of the first rank.' *Philadelphia Inquirer*

'Miss Hepburn ... as fresh and frisky as a puppy out of a tub. She brings a candid innocence and a tomboy intelligence to a part that might have gone sticky, and her performance comes like a breath of fresh air in a stifling season.' Walter Kerr

Ondine (1954)

Cast: Audrey Hepburn (Ondine), Mel Ferrer (The Knight).

Crew: Director: Alfred Lunt.

Story: Based on Jean Giraudoux's fantasy, *Ondine* tells the story of a fifteen-year-old water spirit who, with her androgynous and ethereal beauty, brings destruction to a medieval knight.

Background: The play had been a big pre-Second World War hit in Paris and Mel Ferrer felt that this would be an ideal role for Audrey. So with himself cast as the knight, the play opened on Broadway in February 1954. Audrey, who was the highest-paid actress on Broadway, earning $2,500 per week at this point, received universally acclaimed reviews and won her second Broadway Tony Award for the role. However, all was not as smooth behind the scenes, as rumours circulated that Ferrer (to whom Audrey was now engaged) was pulling rank over the distinguished director, Alfred Lunt, coaching Audrey and demanding that his part be made larger. By opening night, Lunt and Ferrer were not on speaking terms.

Gossip began from this early stage about Ferrer's behaviour with regard to his wife's career. For instance, he refused to allow Audrey to take a solo-bow at the end the play, ensuring that he remained at her side, sharing in her limelight.

The play closed in June 1954 due to Audrey's ill health. She spent the summer in Switzerland recuperating and in September she married the twice-divorced Ferrer. He had two children from his first marriage to Frances Pilchard and two with his second, Barbara Tripp, whom he divorced and married twice.

The Verdict: 'We bought Hepburn and the price was Ferrer. It turned out to be much too expensive.' Anonymous production team member

Audrey once again charmed the critics:

'Ideal from every point of view ... all grace and enchantment, disciplined by an instinct for the realities of theatre.' Brooks Atkinson

However, some were less than thrilled with her on- and off-screen partner:

'[My] only reservation has to do with the performance of Mel Ferrer as the knight-errant ... To my mind, his playing is curiously uninteresting. It lacked vividness, style and imagination almost completely, which is all the more distracting because these are the qualities that the production of *Ondine* possesses so winningly.' Richard Watts Jr, *New York Post*

Anne Frank's Diary (1990/91)

Audrey gave six readings (five in the US and one in the UK) of extracts from Anne Frank's Diary with an orchestral backing composed and conducted by Michael Tilson Thomas. The US performances were performed with the New World Symphony Orchestra. The UK performance was at London's Barbican Centre with the London Symphony Orchestra.

7. How Could They?

Sabrina (1995)

Cast: Julia Ormond (Sabrina), Harrison Ford (Linus Larrabee), Greg Kinnear (David Larrabee), Nancy Marchand (Maude Larrabee), John Wood (Tom Fairchild), Richard Crenna (Patrick Tyson), Angie Dickinson (Ingrid Tyson), Lauren Holly (Elizabeth Tyson, M.D.), Fanny Ardant (Irene).

Crew: Director: Sydney Pollack. Screenplay: David Rayfiel and Barbara Benedek. Cinematography: Giuseppe Rotunno. Music: John Williams.

Story: The basic plot is the same as the original, but with some minor adjustments for a 1990s post-feminist audience. Sabrina (Julia Ormond) is not sent off to Paris to become a cook; she is sent to Paris to work for *Vogue* magazine. Whilst there she is not taken under the wing of a rich baron who remodels her. Here, for fashion and lessons on life and romance, she turns to Irene (Fanny Ardant): for lessons of love and taking photographs she turns to Louis (Patrick Bruel), the photographer at *Vogue*.

In Billy Wilder's *Sabrina Fair*, Mrs Larrabee is rarely seen and doesn't speak. Here there is no Mr Larrabee and it is Maude Larrabee (Nancy Marchand) that runs the company with her son Linus (Harrison Ford) - brother David (Greg Kinnear) is still a wastrel. Maude is a strong, fierce matriarch who rules over her family with an iron fist. Women's roles in films and society have moved on since 1953 as it is not only the Mrs Larrabee role that has altered; Elizabeth Tyson (Lauren Holly), David's fiancée, has emerged forty years on not merely as a pretty young socialite, but as a top paediatrician.

Trivia: Sydney Pollack showed Billy Wilder the final cut of the film. When the lights came up, Pollack waited for the great man's words of wisdom: 'How would you like it if I remade *The Way We Were*?' was his response, as reported in *USA Today*.

The Verdict: A dull and pointless remake as Sydney Pollack adds nothing to Wilder's original, other than heavy-handed political correctness. The cast try their best to break free of the ghostly presence of their predecessors but don't manage it. Greg Kinnear pulls off a passable imitation of William Holden, Harrison Ford comes across as stodgy and dull, and Julia Ormond has the hardest task, as unavoidably she will never be able to compete with The Audrey Hepburn. 2/5

Sabrina Goes To Rome (1998)

Cast: Melissa Joan Hart (Sabrina), Eddie Mills (Paul), Tara Strong (Gwen), James Fields (Travis), Nick Bakay (Salem Saberhagen, the Cat).

Crew: Director: Tibor Takacs. Screenplay: Nell Scovell.

Story: No, not a sequel to the *Sabrina* movies but a remake of *Roman Holiday* featuring everybody's favourite Teenage Witch, Sabrina.

Sabrina (Melissa Joan Hart) goes on a summer vacation to Rome with her cat Salem (Nick Bakay), and shares a room with her distant cousin Gwen (Tara Strong) and her pet guinea pig.

They explore Rome, drinking in the culture and cafe life, and it is in one of the street cafes that they meet two young American students, Paul (Eddie Mills) and Travis (James Fields). They double-date and soon the guys begin to feel there is something strange about Sabrina and Gwen. So with the aid of under-cover surveillance and a video camera, they secretly film Sabrina and Gwen getting up to witch-like antics.

The Verdict: Not actually as bad as it sounds. It's a light bit of fluff that updates the *Roman Holiday* for an audience of teenyboppers that will probably never have seen the original. 3/5

The Audrey Hepburn Story (2000)

Cast: Jennifer Love Hewitt (Audrey Hepburn), Eric McCormack (Mel Ferrer), Frances Fisher (Ella Hepburn), Peter Giles (James Hanson), Keir Dullea (Joseph Hepburn), Gabriel Macht (William Holden), Marcel Jeannin (Givenchy), Michael J Burg (Truman Capote), Emmy Rossum (Teenage Audrey), Sarah Hyland (Young Audrey).

Crew: Director: Steve Robman. Screenplay: Marsha Norman. Cinematography: Pierre Letarte. Music: Lawrence Shragge.

Story: This biopic covers Audrey's life from 1935 to 1960. Using the iconic scene of Audrey Hepburn having breakfast at Tiffany's, the film is told in flash-back, as incidents on the set trigger memories from her past.

Sarah Hyland plays the nine-year-old Audrey, told off for eating pastries. Emmy Rossum plays Audrey at fourteen who is sent to a Kentish boarding school and learns to dance. She then returns to Belgium during the war and acts as a messenger for the Resistance before emerging as Jennifer Love Hewitt at the end of the war, when she returns to England to continue her ballet training before moving into musical theatre and the movies.

Trivia: Unlike the relationship as portrayed here, Truman Capote was as besotted with Audrey Hepburn as the rest of her colleagues. His diaries include many tributes to Audrey over a twenty-year period.

The Verdict: Jennifer Love Hewitt, star and producer, pulls off the complex and demanding role as Audrey Hepburn with great aplomb. Most interesting are Jennifer's recreations of classic Hepburn movie moments including those from *Breakfast At Tiffany's*, *Laughter In Paradise*, *Young Wives' Tale*, *The Lavender Hill Mob*, *Roman Holiday*, *Sabrina Fair* and *The Nun's Story*.

However, the film is excessively glossy and doesn't delve into Hepburn's life in any real depth. Naturally, it uses only the most dramatic portions of her life and dwells on her (non) relationship with her Nazi-sympathiser father. As Audrey refused to talk on the subject, it is a little unclear why this was made the film's central theme. Especially given that the core audience for such a film would either be lovers of Audrey Hepburn or Jennifer Love Hewitt, not necessarily those concerned with Oswald Moseley and the 'Brown Shirts'.

Jennifer is clearly taken with her subject matter and treats it with such reverence that all life is sucked out of both the movie and Audrey Hepburn, leaving a mere replica up on the screen. The film ends with footage of the real Audrey during her UNICEF years and the life and love just shines out, reminding you how special Audrey was and how Jennifer, though a fine actress, can never take her place. 2/5

The Truth About Charlie (2003)

Cast: Thandie Newton (Regina Lampert), Mark Wahlberg (Joshua Peters), Tim Robbins (Mr Bartholomew).

Crew: Director: Jonathan Demme. Screenplay: Peter Stone and Jonathan Demme.

Story: A remake of the 1963 Audrey Hepburn and Cary Grant thriller/comedy/romance *Charade*. The plot has been updated but the main premise remains the same: Regina Lampert is about to get divorced when her husband Charlie dies and all their money goes missing. The mysterious Joshua Peters and a gang of thugs turn up and demand the money that really belongs to them.

Background: At one time, this project was being developed for Will Smith but he jumped ship to appear in Michael Mann's *Ali*.

It was filmed in Paris between March and July 2001 but not released until the summer of 2003. With few post-production special effects, I can only assume that the studio knew they had a dud on their hands.

The Verdict: My sympathies to anyone who has had the misfortune to have seen this truly awful film. A lucky escape went to all those who happened to watch it with me at the Warners in Croydon. I was so tempted to shout out during the film, 'The money is in the...' to have relieved us all from the tedium we were having to endure waiting for the dénouement.

Not only was *The Truth About Charlie* a pointless remake of a flawless movie, but the film's two leads (Mark Wahlberg and Thandie Newton) had no spark between them, leading to a dull 'romance'. Tim Robbins is suitably sinister as Mr Bartholomew, but the gang of thugs is not a patch on the original set.

Its only redeeming feature was the homage to the French New Wave, but even then I'm not quite sure why they were there. Other than the film being shot in Paris, there were no other obvious connections. Nevertheless, cameos by Charles Aznavour as a living manifestation of Peters' seduction technique and Anna Karina as a cabaret performer were welcome relief. Unless you are a French New Wave and Francois Truffaut buff, you might wonder why this old geezer suddenly appears in the lovers' room or why the film's final frame is of Francois Truffaut's headstone. 1/5

Why Can't I Be Audrey Hepburn? (In Production)

Cast: Jennifer Love Hewitt (Perry).

Crew: Director: Ryan Murphy.

Story: A romantic comedy about Perry, a young woman who having reached the age of twenty-five feels that there is more to life than Ohio and moves to Los Angeles. She quickly gets herself a great job and a dashing fiancé. But in one of those 'worst weeks of your life' that only happens in the movies, she gets fired and then dumped (at the altar). In an effort to rebuild her life, she turns to the best man at her wedding, believing that he shares her love of Audrey Hepburn movies. It transpires that he only quotes and references *Breakfast At Tiffany's* to pick up the girls. The bounder. Much like Jack Devlin (Jeremy Northam) picking up Angela Bennett (Sandra Bullock) in *The Net* (1995).

Background: This script has been making the rounds around Hollywood for four years with various young stars attached, including Tea Leoni and Sarah Michelle Gellar. Given Jennifer Love Hewitt's obsession with Audrey Hepburn, this film might now see the light of day.

Breakfast At Tiffany's

Harrison Ford, not content with being involved in the wrecking of one Audrey Hepburn movie, is rumoured to be buying the rights for *Breakfast At Tiffany's* as a possible vehicle for himself and his girlfriend, Calista Flockhart.

I'm only hoping that he is planning on playing the Buddy Ebsen part, not George Peppard's.

8. Audrey Hepburn Inspired Novels

Audrey Hepburn's Neck
by Alan Brown

Pocket Books, 1996

Book Blurb

'Offering a unique perspective and unusual insight into modern Japan and its wartime past, *Audrey Hepburn's Neck* is also a shrewd study of cross-cultural obsessions, and of erotic, romantic and familial love.

'What happens when a young Japanese cartoonist grows up vicariously admiring American culture (and American women) by watching Audrey Hepburn movies as a child and interacting with American expatriates as a young adult? A fascinating novel about romance, sex, and crossing cultural challenges. Alan Brown presents a story seen through the eyes of a young Japanese man, Toshiyuki ('Toshi') Okamoto. He traces his strong attraction to Western women back to his ninth birthday when his mother took him to see Audrey Hepburn in the movie '*Roman Holiday*'. He leaves behind his sad, silent childhood to move to Tokyo to pursue his career in cartooning. There he falls under the spell of three Americans: his best friend and confidante, the generous and extroverted Paul, a gay advertising copywriter who has plenty of his romantic mishaps with Japanese men; Jane, his glamorous but emotionally unstable teacher at the Very Romantic English Academy with whom Toshi has a hazardous sexual affair; and, finally, the lovely and talented composer, Lucy, with whom Toshi falls in love.

'The novel deftly moves back and forth between present and past, as Toshi explores his unhappy childhood, the reasons behind his mother's unexplained abandonment when he was eight years old, and her move to a seaside inn across the peninsula. As the novel draws to a close, tragic events, both public and personal, bring past and present together, revealing the painful truth of Toshi's parents' lives during World War II, and a secret in Toshi's own past that, in the end, gives him the strength and knowledge to confront the future.'

In Beautiful Disguises
by Rajeev Balasubramanyam

Bloomsbury Paperbacks, 2000

Book Blurb

'Life is not easy for a sixteen-year-old girl living in a small-town in South India, especially when she's blessed with a family like hers - an over-dutiful sister, a brother who watches TV as an occupation, a father who drinks and bullies his family, and a silent mother. So when the inevitable marriage arrangement is made, fuelled by dreams and Audrey Hepburn movies, she runs away to The City.

'Secretly hoping she will step right into the shoes of her favourite character, Holly Golightly, she embraces this brave new world with courage, acquiring a taste for croissants and champagne along the way. But she soon realises she can't run forever...'

Best Bit

'Until now, I had seen Hindi films at *Majick Movie House*, and had occasionally watched black and white Kannada or Tamil films on the old television. My father liked these, but I found them boring, too many women crying and they all looked like my mother... though I think this is why my father liked them. But now I watched everything, including English films and comedies. Ravi [her brother] liked them for the naked women, which were plentiful. It seemed that most Americans took their clothes off for no reason at all, and at the most extraordinary time of the day. Anyway, Ravi loved this and I was happy because it proved my theory. But it was through Audrey Hepburn who never took her clothes off, that I learned what film stardom was really about.' pp 17-18

9. Awards

Roman Holiday

Academy Award for Best Actress
New York Film Critics Circle Best Actress
Golden Globe for Best Actress
BAFTA for Best Actress
Picturegoer Gold Medal

Sabrina Fair

Academy Award Nomination for Best Actress
BAFTA Nomination for Best Actress

War And Peace

BAFTA Nomination for Best Actress

The Nun's Story

New York Film Critics Circle Best Actress
BAFTA Best Actress
Zulueta Priza, San Sebastian International Film Festival
Academy Award Nomination for Best Actress

Breakfast At Tiffany's

Academy Award Nomination for Best Actress
Actress of the Year, Film Daily Critics' Poll
Italy's 'Oscar', the Donatello for the best non-Italian actress

Charade

BAFTA Best Actress
Golden Globe Nomination Best Actress

My Fair Lady

Golden Globe Nomination Best Actress

Wait Until Dark

New York Film Critics Circle Best Actress

Golden Globe Nomination Best Actress

Academy Award Nomination for Best Actress

Two For The Road

Golden Globe Nomination Best Actress

Gardens Of The World

Emmy

General

Golden Globe 1955 - World Film Favourite

Cecile B DeMille Award 1990

BAFTA Lifetime Achievement Award in 1992

Screen Actors' Guild Lifetime Achievement Award in 1993

Posthumous recipient of the Jean Hersholt Humanitarian Award at the 1993
Oscars

Her star on the Walk of Fame is at 1650 Vine Street.

10. The Audrey Hepburn Children's Fund

Chairman: Sean Hepburn Ferrer

In 1994, the Audrey Hepburn Children's Fund, a non-profit organisation, was created in New York to continue Audrey's international appeals on behalf of ill-treated and suffering children around the world.

In 1998, the Audrey Hepburn Children's Fund relocated to Los Angeles where it remains today.

The Audrey Hepburn Children's Fund has a growing number of diverse programmes:

Audrey Hepburn Memorial Fund at the US Fund for UNICEF, dedicated to educating children in Somalia, Sudan, Eritrea, Ethiopia and Rwanda.

The first Audrey Hepburn Children's House, located at Hackensack University Medical Centre, offering comprehensive treatment for physically and emotionally abused children in a 'child friendly' environment.

The Audrey Hepburn CARES Team at Children's Hospital, Los Angeles, providing the very best medical and mental health services to suspected victims of child abuse.

'All Children In School' programme, the recently established ten-year joint-venture with the US Fund for UNICEF, aimed at bringing 120,000,000 children worldwide back to school.

Partnership with Casa Alianza, fighting sexual exploitation of children in Central America.

The Fund supports its many diverse programmes through corporate business partnerships, licensing, events, co-ventures with other foundations or institutions and public support.

If you wish to make a donation to the Audrey Hepburn Children's Fund by cheque, money order, or credit card, please do so by addressing your contribution to the Audrey Hepburn Children's Fund:

Audrey Hepburn Children's Fund
710 Wilshire Blvd., Suite 600
Santa Monica, CA 90401

www.audreyhepburn.com

11. Reference Materials

Books On Audrey Hepburn

A Star Danced: The Life Of Audrey Hepburn by Robyn Karney, 1993, Bloomsbury

Adieu Audrey by Klaus-Jürgen Semback, 1995, Neues Publishing Co.

Audrey - The Life Of Audrey Hepburn by Charles Higham, 1984, Macmillian Publishing Co.

Audrey Hepburn - A Biography by Warren G Harris, 1994, Simon & Schuster

Audrey Hepburn: An Elegant Spirit by Sean Hepburn Ferrer, 2003, Sidgwick & Jackson

Audrey Hepburn - An Intimate Portrait by Diana Maychick, 1996, Carol Publishing Group

Audrey Hepburn by Barry Paris, 2000, Orion

Audrey Hepburn by Ian Woodward, 1984, W H Allen

Audrey Hepburn, 1999, Electra/Art Books International

Audrey Hepburn: A Celebration by Sheridan Morley, 1993, Pavilion

Audrey Hepburn: A Life In Pictures by Carol Krenz, 1997, Friedman/Fairfax Pub.

Audrey Style by Pamela Clarke Keogh, 1999, HarperCollins

Audrey: Her Real Story by Alexander Walker, 2000, Orion (revised and updated version)

Cecil Beaton's 'Fair Lady' by Cecil Beaton, 1964, Weidenfeld and Nicolson

Complete Films Of Audrey Hepburn, The by Jerry Vermilye, 1997, Carol Publishing Group

Growing Up With Audrey Hepburn: Text, Audience, Resonance (Inside Popular Film) by Rachel Mosely, 2003, Manchester University Press

Books Referenced

All The Devils Are Here by David Seabrook, 2000, Granta

Gardens Of The World: The Art And Practice Of Gardening edited by Penelope Hobhouse & Elvin McDonald, 1991, Macmillan

Getting Away With It or: The Further Adventures Of The Luckiest Bastard You Ever Saw. Starring Steven Soderbergh. Also starring Richard Lester as The Man Who Knew More Than He Was Asked, 1999, Faber & Faber

Self Portrait With Friends: The Selected Diaries Of Cecil Beaton edited by Richard Buckle, 1979, Pimlico

The Brief, Madcap Life Of Kay Kendall by Eve Golden (with Kim Kendall), 2002, University Press of Kentucky

The Dress Doctor by Edith Head, 1959, The World's Work

The Noel Coward Diaries edited by Graham Payne and Sheridan Morley, 1982, Macmillan

Videos And DVDs

DVD Region 1 (Starring Audrey Hepburn)

Always

Breakfast At Tiffany's

Charade

Children's Hour, The

Funny Face Special Features: Retrospective Featurette: 'Paramount In The 1950's'

Gardens Of The World With Audrey Hepburn

Lavender Hill Mob, The

Love In The Afternoon

My Fair Lady Special Features: Feature length audio commentary, behind the scenes documentary, alternative Audrey Hepburn vocal versions of 'Show Me' and 'Wouldn't It Be Loverly?', production notes and four theatrical trailers.

Robin And Marian

Paris When It Sizzles

Roman Holiday Special Features: 'Remembering *Roman Holiday*' featurette, 'Edith Head: The Paramount Years' featurette and 'Restoring *Roman Holiday*' featurette.

Sabrina Special Features: Retrospective documentary on the making of '*Sabrina*'.

Unforgiven, The

Wait Until Dark

War And Peace Special Features: Theatrical trailer, re-release trailer and 'Behind the scenes' of '*War And Peace*'.

DVD Region 1 (Related DVDs)

Love Goddesses, The (documentary)

Sabrina (1995)

Truth About Charlie, The, Special Features: Feature commentary, deleted scenes and 'making-of' featurette.

DVD Region 2 (Starring Audrey Hepburn)

Always

Audrey Hepburn Box Set (Includes: *Breakfast At Tiffany's, Funny Face, Sabrina Fair* and *Paris When It Sizzles*)

Breakfast At Tiffany's

Charade

Ealing Comedy Collection (Includes: *The Ladykillers, The Lavender Hill Mob, The Man In The White Suit* and *Kind Hearts And Coronets*)

Family Films Box Set B (Includes*: Charade, The Millionairess, At War With The Army* and *Road To Bali*)

Funny Face

Gardens Of The World With Audrey Hepburn

Lavender Hill Mob, The

My Fair Lady Special Features: Audio commentary featuring key members of the restoration team, trailer and 'behind the scenes' footage.

Paris When It Sizzles

Robin And Marian

Roman Holiday Special Features: 'Remembering *Roman Holiday*' featurette, 'Edith Head: The Paramount Years' featurette and 'Restoring *Roman Holiday*' featurette.

Sabrina Fair Special Features: Retrospective documentary on the making of 'Sabrina Fair'.

DVD Region 2 (Related DVDs)

Audrey Hepburn Story, The

Hollywood Musicals Of The 1960s (documentary)

Love Goddesses, The (documentary)

Sabrina (1995)

Truth About Charlie, The

NTSC VHS

Always
Breakfast At Tiffany's
Charade
Children's Hour, The
Funny Face
Gardens Of The World With Audrey Hepburn
Green Mansions
How To Steal A Million
Lavender Hill Mob, The
Love In The Afternoon
My Fair Lady
Nun's Story, The
One Wild Oat
Paris When It Sizzles
Robin And Marian
Roman Holiday
Sabrina
Sidney Sheldon's Bloodline
They All Laughed
Two For The Road
Unforgiven, The
Wait Until Dark
War And Peace

PAL VHS

Always
Breakfast At Tiffany's
Charade
Funny Face
Gardens Of The World With Audrey Hepburn
Lavender Hill Mob, The
My Fair Lady
Nun's Story, The
Paris When It Sizzles
Robin And Marian
Roman Holiday
Sabrina Fair
Wait Until Dark
War And Peace

Websites

http://www.audreyhepburn.com
http://www.geocities.com/classicallyaudrey/
http://www.geocities.com/audreyhepburnunicef/
http://www.angelfire.com/alt/fabaudrey/
http://www.geocities.com/Hollywood/Film/1907/simply_audrey.html
http://www.audreyhepburn.org/grahamspage

Documentaries

My Lady hosted by Jeremy Brett, BBC TV
Then And Now: The Making Of My Fair Lady (on VHS release), 1994
Audrey Hepburn Remembered, BBC TV
Biography: Audrey Hepburn, History Channel
Hollywood Greats: Audrey Hepburn, BBC TV
Omnibus: My Fair Lady, BBC TV
The Bike's The Star: The Vespa, BBC TV

The Essential Library: History Best-Sellers

Build up your library with new titles published every month

Conspiracy Theories by Robin Ramsay, £3.99

Do you think *The X-Files* is fiction? That Elvis is dead? That the US actually went to the moon? And don't know that the ruling elite did a deal with the extra-terrestrials after the Roswell crash in 1947... At one time, you could blame the world's troubles on the Masons or the Illuminati, or the Jews, or One Worlders, or the Great Communist Conspiracy. Now we also have the alien-US elite conspiracy, or the alien shape-shifting reptile conspiracy to worry about - and there are books to prove it as well! This book tries to sort out the handful of wheat from the choking clouds of intellectual chaff. For among the nonsensical Conspiracy Theory rubbish currently proliferating on the Internet, there are important nuggets of real research about real conspiracies waiting to be mined.

The Rise Of New Labour by Robin Ramsay, £3.99

The rise of New Labour? How did that happen? As everybody knows, Labour messed up the economy in the 1970s, went too far to the left, became 'unelectable' and let Mrs Thatcher in. After three General Election defeats Labour modernised, abandoned the left and had successive landslide victories in 1997 and 2001.

That's the story they print in newspapers. The only problem is...the real story of the rise of New Labour is more complex, and it involves the British and American intelligence services, the Israelis and elite management groups like the Bilderbergers.

Robin Ramsay untangles the myths and shows how it really happened that Gordon Brown sank gratefully into the arms of the bankers, Labour took on board the agenda of the City of London, and that nice Mr Blair embraced his role as the last dribble of Thatcherism down the leg of British politics.

UFOs by Neil Nixon, £3.99

UFOs and Aliens have been reported throughout recorded time. Reports of UFO incidents vary from lights in the sky to abductions. The details are frequently terrifying, always baffling and occasionally hilarious. This book includes the best-known cases, the most incredible stories and the answers that explain them. There are astounding and cautionary tales which suggest that the answers we seek may be found in the least likely places.

The Essential Library: History Best-Sellers

Build up your library with new titles published every month

Ancient Greece by Mike Paine, £3.99

Western civilization began with the Greeks. From the highpoint of the 5th century BC through the cultural triumphs of the Alexandrian era to their impact on the developing Roman empire, the Greeks shaped the philosophy, art, architecture and literature of the Mediterranean world. Mike Paine provides a concise and well-informed narrative of many centuries of Greek history. He highlights the careers of great political and military leaders like Pericles and Alexander the Great, and shows the importance of the great philosophers like Plato and Aristotle. Dramatists and demagogues, stoics and epicureans, aristocrats and helots take their places in the unfolding story of the Greek achievement.

Black Death by Sean Martin, £3.99

The Black Death is the name most commonly given to the pandemic of bubonic plague that ravaged the medieval world in the late 1340s. From Central Asia the plague swept through Europe, leaving millions of dead in its wake. Between a quarter and a third of Europe's population died. In England the population fell from nearly six million to just over three million. The Black Death was the greatest demographic disaster in European history.

American Civil War by Phil Davies, £3.99

The American Civil War, fought between North and South in the years 1861-1865, was the bloodiest and most traumatic war in American history. Rival visions of the future of the United States faced one another across the battlefields and families and friends were bitterly divided by the conflict. This book examines the deep-rooted causes of the war, so much more complicated than the simple issue of slavery.

American Indian Wars by Howard Hughes, £3.99

At the beginning of the 1840s the proud tribes of the North American Indians looked across the plains at the seemingly unstoppable expansion of the white man's West. During the decades of conflict that followed, as the new world pushed onward, the Indians saw their way of life disappear before their eyes. Over the next 40 years they clung to a dream of freedom and a continuation of their traditions, a dream that was repeatedly shattered by the whites.

The Essential Library: Film Best-Sellers

Build up your library with new titles every month

Film Noir (Revised & Updated Edition) by Paul Duncan

The laconic private eye, the corrupt cop, the heist that goes wrong, the femme fatale with the rich husband and the dim lover - these are the trademark characters of Film Noir. This book charts the progression of the Noir style as a vehicle for film-makers who wanted to record the darkness at the heart of American society as it emerged from World War to the Cold War. As well as an introduction explaining the origins of Film Noir, seven films are examined in detail and an exhaustive list of over 500 Films Noirs are listed.

Alfred Hitchcock (Revised & Updated Edition) by Paul Duncan

More than 20 years after his death, Alfred Hitchcock is still a household name, most people in the Western world have seen at least one of his films, and he popularised the action movie format we see every week on the cinema screen. He was both a great artist and dynamite at the box office. This book examines the genius and enduring popularity of one of the most influential figures in the history of the cinema!

Orson Welles (Revised & Updated Edition) by Martin Fitzgerald

The popular myth is that after the artistic success of *Citizen Kane* it all went downhill for Orson Welles, that he was some kind of fallen genius. Yet, despite overwhelming odds, he went on to make great Films Noirs like *The Lady From Shanghai* and *Touch Of Evil*. He translated Shakespeare's work into films with heart and soul (*Othello*, *Chimes At Midnight*, *Macbeth*), and he gave voice to bitterness, regret and desperation in *The Magnificent Ambersons* and *The Trial*. Far from being down and out, Welles became one of the first cutting-edge independent film-makers.

Woody Allen (Revised & Updated Edition) by Martin Fitzgerald

Woody Allen: Neurotic. Jewish. Funny. Inept. Loser. A man with problems. Or so you would think from the characters he plays in his movies. But hold on. Allen has written and directed 30 films. He may be a funny man, but he is also one of the most serious American film-makers of his generation. This revised and updated edition includes *Sweet And Lowdown* and *Small Time Crooks*.

Stanley Kubrick (Revised & Updated Edition) by Paul Duncan

Kubrick's work, like all masterpieces, has a timeless quality. His vision is so complete, the detail so meticulous, that you believe you are in a three-dimensional space displayed on a two-dimensional screen. He was commercially successful because he embraced traditional genres like War (*Paths Of Glory, Full Metal Jacket*), Crime (*The Killing*), Science Fiction (*2001*), Horror (*The Shining*) and Love (*Barry Lyndon*). At the same time, he stretched the boundaries of film with controversial themes: underage sex (*Lolita*); ultra violence (*A Clockwork Orange*); and erotica (*Eyes Wide Shut*).

The Essential Library: Recent Film Releases

Build up your library with new titles every month

Tim Burton by Colin Odell & Michelle Le Blanc

Tim Burton makes films about outsiders on the periphery of society. His heroes are psychologically scarred, perpetually naive and childlike, misunderstood or unintentionally disruptive. They upset convential society and morality. Even his villains are rarely without merit - circumstance blurs the divide between moral fortitude and personal action. But most of all, his films have an aura of the fairytale, the fantastical and the magical.

French New Wave by Chris Wiegand

The directors of the French New Wave were the original film geeks - a collection of celluloid-crazed cinéphiles with a background in film criticism and a love for American auteurs. Having spent countless hours slumped in Parisian cinémathèques, they armed themselves with handheld cameras, rejected conventions, and successfully moved movies out of the studios and on to the streets at the end of the 1950s.

Borrowing liberally from the varied traditions of film noir, musicals and science fiction, they released a string of innovative and influential pictures, including the classics *Jules Et Jim* and *A Bout De Souffle*. By the mid-1960s, the likes of Jean-Luc Godard, François Truffaut, Claude Chabrol, Louis Malle, Eric Rohmer and Alain Resnais had changed the rules of film-making forever.

Bollywood by Ashok Banker

Bombay's prolific Hindi-language film industry is more than just a giant entertainment juggernaut for 1 billion-plus Indians worldwide. It's a part of Indian culture, language, fashion and lifestyle. It's also a great bundle of contradictions and contrasts, like India itself. Thrillers, horror, murder mysteries, courtroom dramas, Hong Kong-style action gunfests, romantic comedies, soap operas, mythological costume dramas... they're all blended with surprising skill into the musical boy-meets-girl formula of Bollywood. This vivid introduction to Bollywood, written by a Bollywood scriptwriter and media commentator, examines 50 major films in entertaining and intimate detail.

Mike Hodges by Mark Adams

Features an extensive interview with Mike Hodges. His first film, *Get Carter*, has achieved cult status (recently voted the best British film ever in *Hotdog* magazine) and continues to be the benchmark by which every British crime film is measured. His latest film, *Croupier*, was such a hit in the US that is was re-issued in the UK. His work includes crime drama (*Pulp*), science-fiction (*Flash Gordon* and *The Terminal Man*), comedy (*Morons From Outer Space*) and watchable oddities such as *A Prayer For The Dying* and *Black Rainbow*. Mike Hodges is one of the great maverick British filmmakers.

The Essential Library: Currently Available

Film Directors:

Woody Allen (2nd)	Tim Burton	Ang Lee
Jane Campion*	John Carpenter	Joel & Ethan Coen (2nd)
Jackie Chan	Steven Soderbergh	Clint Eastwood
David Cronenberg	Terry Gilliam*	Michael Mann
Alfred Hitchcock (2nd)	Krzysztof Kieslowski*	Roman Polanski
Stanley Kubrick (2nd)	Sergio Leone	Oliver Stone
David Lynch (2nd)	Brian De Palma*	George Lucas
Sam Peckinpah*	Ridley Scott (2nd)	James Cameron
Orson Welles (2nd)	Billy Wilder	Roger Corman
Steven Spielberg	Mike Hodges	Spike Lee
Hal Hartley		

Film Genres:

Blaxploitation Films	Bollywood	French New Wave
Horror Films	Spaghetti Westerns	Vietnam War Movies
Slasher Movies	Film Noir	Hammer Films
Vampire Films*	Heroic Bloodshed*	Carry On Films
German Expressionist Films		

Film Subjects:

Laurel & Hardy	Marx Brothers	Film Music
Steve McQueen*	Marilyn Monroe	The Oscars® (2nd)
Filming On A Microbudget	Bruce Lee	Writing A Screenplay
Film Studies		

Music:

The Madchester Scene	Beastie Boys	Jethro Tull
How To Succeed In The Music Business		The Beatles

Literature:

Cyberpunk	Philip K Dick	The Beat Generation
Agatha Christie	Sherlock Holmes	Noir Fiction
Terry Pratchett	Hitchhiker's Guide (2nd)	Alan Moore
William Shakespeare	Creative Writing	Tintin
Georges Simenon	Robert Crumb	

Ideas:

Conspiracy Theories	Nietzsche	UFOs
Feminism	Freud & Psychoanalysis	Bisexuality

History:

Alchemy & Alchemists	The Crusades	The Black Death
Jack The Ripper	The Rise Of New Labour	Ancient Greece
American Civil War	American Indian Wars	Witchcraft
Globalisation	Who Shot JFK?	Videogaming
Classic Radio Comedy	Nuclear Paranoia	

Miscellaneous:

Stock Market Essentials	How To Succeed As A Sports Agent	Doctor Who

Available at bookstores or send a cheque (payable to 'Oldcastle Books') to: **Pocket Essentials (Dept AU), P O Box 394, Harpenden, Herts, AL5 1XJ, UK**. £3.99 each (£2.99 if marked with an *). For each book add 50p (UK)/£1 (elsewhere) postage & packing.